Miró

Beatrix Potter

Virginia Woolf

Edvard Munch

Mark Twain

C. M. Russell

ROBE GOLDBERG

1916

Victor Hugo

Paul Gauguin

E. B.   9.
18   64

Salvador Dalí
1952

Baudelaire

P. Signac

The Illustrated Letter

The Illustrated Letter

Charles Hamilton

Universe Books
New York

To

Susan Miller

who helped enormously in the
birth of this book

———————————

Published in the United States of America in 1987
by Universe Books
381 Park Avenue South, New York, NY 10016

87 88 89 90 91 / 10 9 8 7 6 5 4 3 2 1

Designed by Rosing & Rosing

Printed in the United States of America

Library of Congress Cataloging-in-Publication Data

The Illustrated Letter

Includes index.
1. Letters—Manuscripts—Facsimiles.
I. Hamilton, Charles, 1913–
PN6131.I45 1987   700'.92'2   87-16184
ISBN 0-87663-664-4

Contents

Preface

What American author tacked a picture note on his front door telling burglars how to rob his home? Mark Twain, of course, who also added explicit instructions not to wake him up.

What African explorer posted the ultimate, vulgar insult to a fellow academician who had questioned his facts? Sir Richard F. Burton—and he did it without writing a single word.

What English novelist was so clever at getting out of boring dinner dates that he never once offended a would-be host? None other than W. M. Thackeray, who even delighted a French count with his penned rebuffs.

These amusing, illustrated notes, together with about one hundred others by great painters like Vincent van Gogh and Picasso and talented amateurs like O. Henry and Theodore Roosevelt, brighten the pages of this book. Despite the disparity in their artistic skills, they all knew how to draw pictures in their letters to put across a message or tell a story. And, without exception, they have now set their pens to the pleasant task of entertaining you.

This unique assemblage of pictorial notes got its start forty years ago when I bought a rebus letter of J. Goldsborough Bruff, famed as the artist of the Gold Rush. Bruff's letter was filled with tiny drawings, each of which represented a syllable or a word. You'll find his letter here and I hope you have as much fun deciphering it as I did. My delight in this quaint missive launched me on a quest for other illustrated notes. For years I haunted museums and libraries and reconnoitered manuscript archives. I seized upon every pictorial epistle that wafted into my ken. I beseeched my friends for copies of treasures in their files and let it be known, far and wide, in America and Europe, that I was in pursuit of picture notes.

Now, four decades later, I am at last able to place before you an imposing gallery of illustrated letters.

The Illustrated Letter

Princess Louise of Bohemia was born about 1625. Her father was Frederick V (1596–1632), elector Palatine of the Rhine and king of Bohemia, whose wife was Elizabeth, daughter of King James I of England. Frederick was crowned king of Bohemia in 1619, but one year later his reign abruptly ended when his army was routed near Prague by the Catholic League forces commanded by Tilly. Frederick died in exile at Mainz.

This rebus letter exhibits both wit and artistry. The rebus, as the princess facetiously explains to her correspondent (probably her brother and no doubt the booted viol player who asks in a foreign accent, "What shall wee singa?"), is partly in drawings to make the English text more intelligible.

It is a challenge to decipher Louise's pictographs. In perusing the English text and the French note at the bottom, the reader should bear in mind that the Jacobean letter *e* can easily be mistaken for a *t* or an *r*. The first line and a half may be deciphered: "*Eye* (I) have received *urn* (yourn) *letter* by my La *dice* (ladies') Li *bell* (libel)ing my *Friend* (a Quaker, at this period known as a Friend)." The last phrase in the letter reads: "meane *time* (an hourglass with wings) *eye* (I) re *mane* . . ."

And now I pass the challenge on to you.

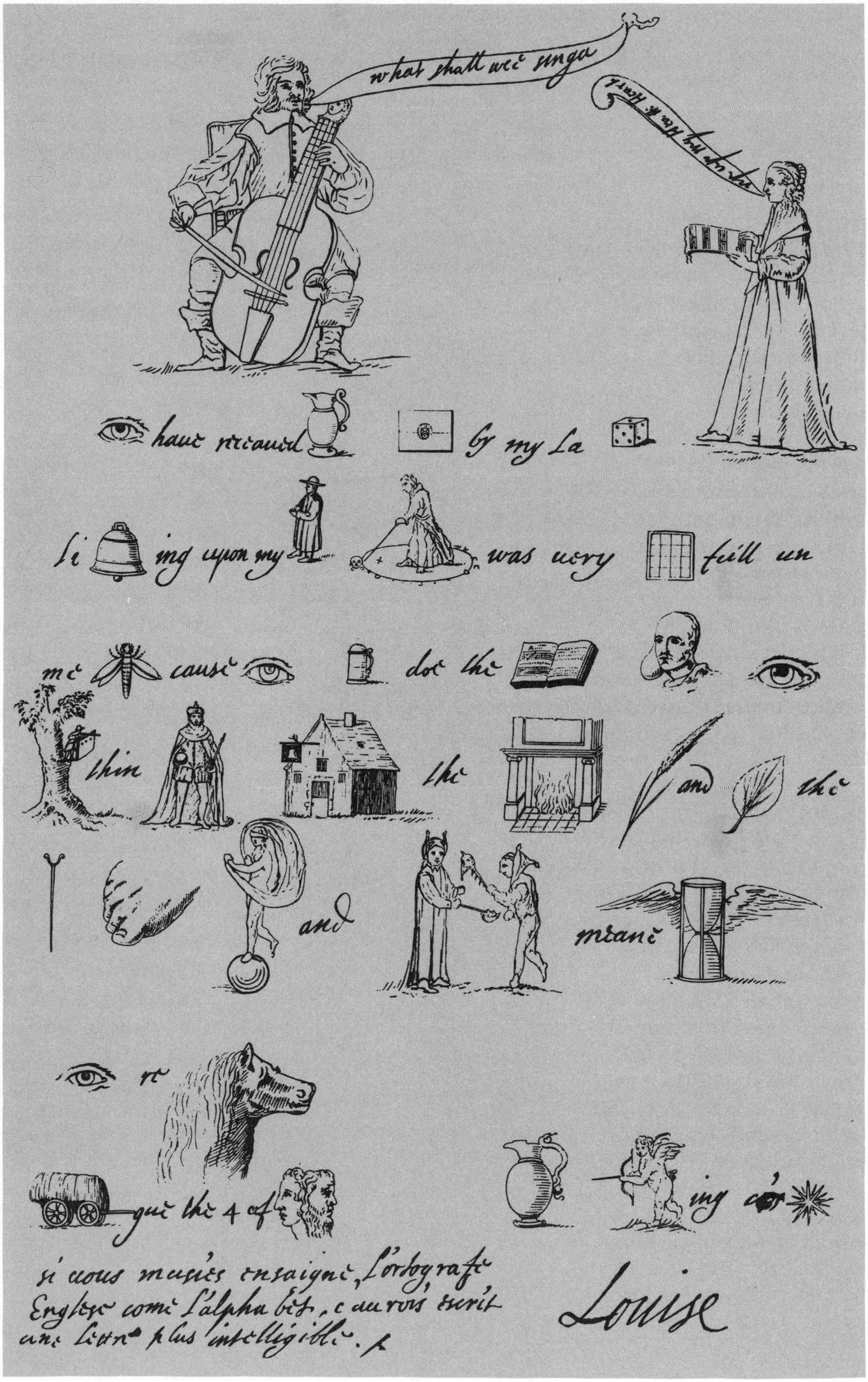

Benjamin Franklin

(1706–90), often called "the first civilized American," began his great career in his brother's printing shop in Boston. In his famous *Autobiography*, Franklin has recounted the story of his early life, but his later achievements and adventures are far more spectacular. He invented and experimented with bifocal lenses for spectacles, a new type of stove, musical glasses, lightning rods, and a dozen other useful gadgets. He originated our modern postal system. As a polemical writer he rivaled Thomas Paine. His diplomatic skills won French support for the American Revolution. Franklin was immensely popular in France, where he lived for nine years. It is said that he had a mistress on every street in Paris, probably a record for a septuagenarian. Among Franklin's achievements, he helped to write, then signed, the Declaration of Independence; with John Jay and John Adams he negotiated the treaty with England that ended the Revolutionary War; and he was president of Pennsylvania (1785–87). One of his last acts was to sign a memorial to Congress that urged the abolition of slavery.

Franklin was the complete Renaissance man—author, statesman, inventor, scientist, musician, accomplished lover, champion of liberty, and—just incidentally—the first American master of a new art form, the illustrated letter.

In this letter to a fellow scientist, Franklin sends "A Magical Circle of Circles" that illustrates another facet of his inventive genius.

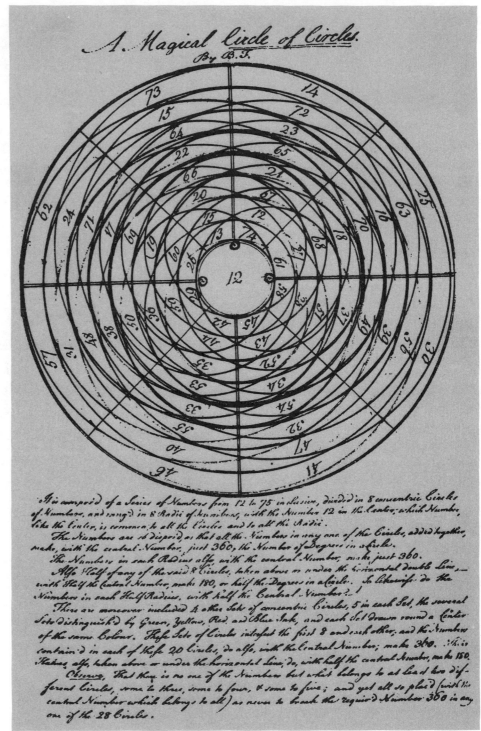

Mark Twain was the pen moniker that Samuel Langhorne Clemens (1835–1910) took from an old expression used by pilots and boat hands while sounding on the Mississippi. Born in Florida, Missouri, he started his career as a mischievous boy, later setting down his real and imaginary adventures in *Tom Sawyer.* Twain was never plagued or disturbed by formal education. He was a printer's devil at twelve, and later a steamboat pilot on the Mississippi until the Civil War in 1861 put an end to the river traffic. After a few hectic days in the Confederate army, Twain deserted and set out for Nevada. He tried mining and failed at it. But he was an immediate hit as an author, and his tale of a jumping frog that couldn't jump because it was loaded with buckshot won him a wide audience. With every book he wrote the audience got bigger, and by the time of his death Twain was the most celebrated and beloved author in the world.

The letter addressed to Mark's wife Livy (Olivia Langdon Clemens) is a charming rebus penned just for his children. The "Notice. To the next Burglar" was hand-lettered and signed by Clemens and posted on his front door after a midnight thief broke into his home. The thief was quickly apprehended because he had trouble making a getaway with a heavy sack of silver.

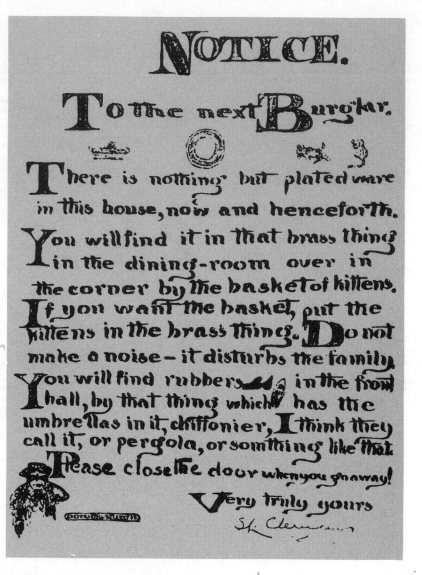

Montrea[l], ☼ day,   27, 1881

(The blank means that there is no vem-
ber there.)

Livy

——— ,   A 🐍 kept me awake

night till 3 or 4 o' [clock] — so

[eye] am lying a-[sofa] this morning

I would [rather] give

yonder in the

although it is only snow.

There. — that's for the children
— was not sure that they could read
writing, especially Jean, who is strangely
ignorant in some things.   Mark Twain

Nothing is known of **John D. Wilkins** except that, like dozens of other soldiers, Union and Confederate, he wrote letters home from the front lines. Occasionally the men of the blue and gray enhanced their letters with sketches. Here Union officer Wilkins sends a meditative self-portrait from "the Camp near Chancellorsville, Va., May 5th, 1863" and reports that "the fighting still progresses." Wilkins did not know that even as he wrote, the great Confederate soldier Thomas Jonathan "Stonewall" Jackson lay close to death after being accidentally shot by his own men.

David Dixon Porter (1813–91), a daring and skillful American naval officer, was the son of Captain David Porter, hero of Tripoli and the War of 1812. When his foster brother David G. Farragut was made commander of the entire Union navy, Porter was put in charge of a mortar flotilla and from that time on took a heated part in nearly every important naval action of the war. He helped Grant in the capture of Vicksburg.

In this abbreviated, gossipy letter to his brother-in-law Gwinn Harris Heap, a Western explorer, Porter makes a duck-to-rooster sketch of Farragut, depicting the admiral before and after he aided in the capture of New Orleans. He than portrays himself in the act of giving a brazen salute, ready to be fired out of one of the mortars he was soon to use with terrifying effect upon the enemy at Vicksburg (28 June 1862), only three weeks after this letter was penned.

Eugene Field

(1850–95), the beloved poet of childhood who wrote "Little Boy Blue" and "Wynken, Blynken and Nod," was also a maestro of colored inks and uncial initials. His original manuscripts, indited in jet black ink in a fastidious, tiny script, are calligraphic masterpieces, often illuminated in brilliant inks of blue, gold, bronze, green, and red.

After an erratic college education, during which he acquired an arcane knowledge of the classics, Field traveled in Europe and lavished away a small inheritance. He settled down as a columnist in his birthplace, St. Louis, Missouri, but later moved to Chicago, where his irreverent squibs and sentimental impromptus won him wide acclaim.

18

Field was renowned for his practical jokes. Many of his whimsical letters describe amusing events that never occurred or laud nonexistent books. His epistles, often adorned with sketches, are full of merry jests, a delight to look upon and read.

In this quaint letter to "Nomp" (Field's friend and biographer Slason Thompson), the poet describes a baseball game with exaggerated enthusiasm.

O. Henry took the sordid and tawdry side of life in New York City and transformed it into the magic world of "Baghdad on the Subway." With superb imagination and keen humor he turned out story after story, almost always with a surprise twist. The tragedy of his own life, which included three years in prison for a crime he probably did not commit, gave him a deep sympathy and understanding for the luckless clerk or shop girl often trapped by fate. Like his French counterpart, Guy de Maupassant, O. Henry is frequently criticized by fashion-conscious, highbrow critics for his contrived plots and surprise endings, but his style is always lucid, his narrative skill unimpeachable, and his characterization brilliant.

O. Henry's real name was William Sydney Porter (1862–1910). He was born in Greensboro, North Carolina, and quit school at fifteen to work for five years as a clerk in his uncle's drug store. The next few years found him moving from job to job: rancher in Texas, bookkeeper in a land office, writer and editor, and teller in a bank. It was the last job that got him into trouble. He was accused of embezzling $1,150 and would have been acquitted, except that he got scared and fled to Honduras. When he eventually returned to Austin, Texas, where his wife lay dying, he was arrested, tried, and sentenced to five years' imprisonment in the Ohio State Penitentiary. Here he began writing the stories, many of them about con men or Texas cowhands, that brought him fame under the pseudynom O(liver), Henry.

I own an old and rare phonograph record of O. Henry chatting about himself. He notes, in reference to his "twist" story endings, that "the unusual is the ordinary, rather than the unexpected." And he concludes by saying, in a soft and beguiling Southern accent: "Ah hope that this little talk will be heard long after Ah'm gone, and Ah want you-all to continue readin' my stories then, too. Goodbye, folks."

O. Henry loved to caricature himself. On the postcard of the Flatiron Building he salutes an old pal by shaking hands with him across the top floor.

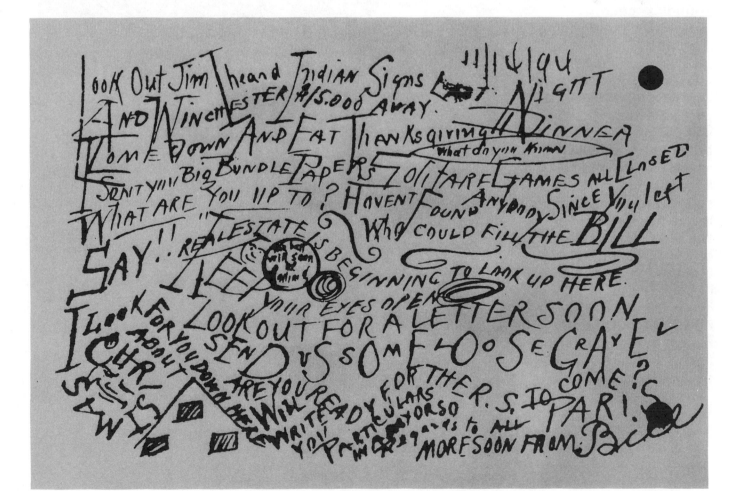

Theodore Roosevelt (1858–1919), twenty-sixth president of the United States, a fearless man of boundless energy and gusto, with a sharp mind that probed into almost every area of knowledge, was a nonstop letter writer who kept his friends—and enemies—under a constant state of epistolary bombardment. His explosive letters, often typewritten but peppered with manuscript corrections, are invariably interesting. Whether Teddy expostulates on politics or hunting or human rights, he never dodges an issue, and his comments are always forthright and bluff. He held nothing of himself back and poured his very psyche into his letters.

WHITE HOUSE,
WASHINGTON.

March 29th 1905

Blessed little Sheffield

Your aunt Edith and I have felt dreadfully sorry about you; and so have Quentin and Archie and Ethel. I hope you are feeling a little better now. Kermit says I ought to send you a picture letter, because my children used to like to get one,

After breakfast each morning your
aunt Edith and I walk in
the garden with Jack

Aunt Edith
(after Miss Beaux)

Uncle Theodore

Jack

Jack chases a squirrel

which goes up a tree, &
leaves Jack barking below.

jack encounters a cat in a bush

jack barking

cat bush.

the cat escapes through the fence

we meet Quentin dragging a wagon

The notes he wrote to his children are little classics. Full of spontaneous warmth, they are also adorned with hasty but delightful sketches that reveal the artistic facet of his genius. Just before his death, Teddy said of the letters he wrote to his children: "I would rather have them published than anything that has ever been written about me."

The picture letter, as he calls it, is to his nephew Sheffield.

Achie appears with a bow
and arrows.

Then we go into the house

Your loving
Uncle Theodore

A game of tennis

Kermit   Uncle Theodore

Booth Tarkington

(1869–1946), one of the most versatile of American authors, was born in Indianapolis, Indiana, and prepped at Phillips Exeter Academy. He attended Purdue for a short time, then transferred to Princeton, from which he was graduated in 1893. His novel *The Gentleman from Indiana* (1899) won him early fame. He followed this with *Monsieur Beaucaire* (1900), a comic tale of an 18th-century barber. Tarkington's humorous portrayal of a Midwest boyhood, *Penrod* (1914), is a story of the magic and wonder of adolescence.

In the letter to "Dear Wells," Tarkington elatedly announces the completion of a book. In contrast is the blistering fury when presented with a postage-due parcel that unexpectedly turned out to be a bottle of cocktails.

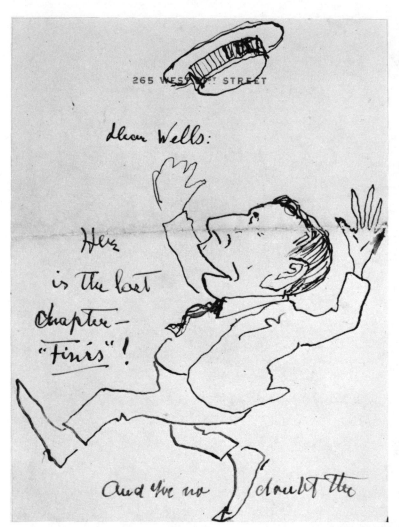

265 WEST ?? STREET

Dear Wells:

Here is the last Chapter — "Finis"!

And I've no doubt the

relief in the office will be as great as my own — that at least, it's all *done*!

And will you send me ~~those~~ proofs as soon as possible. I have about everything ready for the book copy. And may I have a set also of the corrected (or page proofs) of the October installment to go over again for the book? And any proofs of the later pictures of Hilshovski?

Hastily

W. ??

F. Scott Fitzgerald

(1896–1940), named after the author of "The Star-Spangled Banner," lived a star-spangled life, crammed with outrageous folly and frenetic excitement. He belonged to the flapper era and the wild 'twenties and wrote about the people of that time, their crazed pleasures and ultimate disillusionment. Born in Minnesota, Fitzgerald studied at Princeton, the scene of his first novel, *This Side of Paradise,* a cynical scrutiny of the youth of the jazz age. The book established Fitzgerald as a brilliant wit and a major writer. In 1925 he wrote *The Great Gatsby,* a tale of postwar times when orgies were regarded as marks of success. Fitzgerald's later works, some of them ground out in an alcoholic haze, reflect the disintegration of the author and the world he wrote about.

In this letter, the text of which is somewhat shortened, Fitzgerald tells his artist, Arthur William Brown, how to illustrate his story of The Caddy.

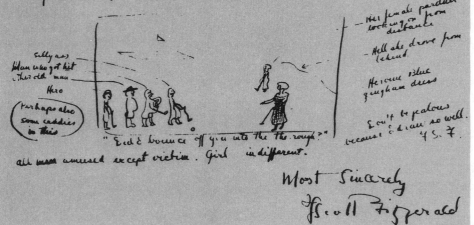

28

Jacob Bell

(1810–59), while working with his father as a chemist on Oxford Street in London, attended chemistry lectures at the Royal Institute and medical courses at King's College. He quickly became aware that many of the practices in mixing and dispensing drugs were at least a century out of date and began to search for methods of improving the practice of pharmacy. In 1831 he founded The Pharmaceutical Society of Great Britain. He also established, and for eighteen years edited, *The Pharmaceutical Journal.* In 1850 Bell was elected to parliament from St. Albans. He introduced a bill, part of which subsequently became law, to standardize pharmaceutical procedures and curb the practice of pharmacy by unqualified persons.

This clever rebus letter suggests that Bell's talents were not confined to pharmacy.

William Makepeace Thackeray (1811–63)

cried "Go to!" when Charles Dickens turned down his application to illustrate *Pickwick Papers.* "If Dickens doesn't want me to draw the pictures for *his* book, I'll write my own books and then illustrate them myself." And that is precisely what Thackeray did. A succession of clever burlesques and character probes from his pen, all bearing his lively drawings, culminated ten years later in *Vanity Fair,* an illustrated novel that put Thackeray on a literary par with his amiable rival Dickens.

The artist-turned-novelist had begun his career at Trinity College, Cambridge, where his wit and wisdom won him a wide circle of friends. At 21 he inherited a small fortune, but some unwise investments, including a few disastrous sessions at the gaming table, stripped him of his modest wealth. From then on, it was Thackeray's quill that supported him.

Thackeray's novels are rich in pathos and humor, but his artistic sallies are almost equally brilliant. Under a variety of quaint pen names he bombarded hs friends with letters, many of them enlivened with caricatures. The catalog of Thackeray's comic pseudonyms is too long for recounting, but here are a few: Michael Angelo Titmarsh, Charles James Yellowplush, George Savage Fitzboodle, and Theophile Wagstaff. Often Thackeray signed his notes merely with initials or not at all, for there wasn't one of his friends who failed to recognize instantly his distinctive chirography. Mr. Titmarsh's favorite subject for satire was his own visage, solemn and bespectacled.

I doubt if anyone who got a missive from Thackeray, indited in his concise and beautiful script and adorned with delightful sketches, ever pitched it away or used it to light a fire.

In the first letter, Mr. Tit-marsh (Thackeray), with his "foot actually uplifted to quit the shore of Albion," agrees to turn back to accept an invitation. The following brace of letters was no doubt written to the clever, unbiquitous bon vivant, Count Alfred d'Orsay. In the final letter, Thackeray apologizes to Mrs. Eliot for not meeting one of her friends. ". . . the little printer's devil barred my door and I could not come out."

My dear Madam

It was as I feared on Friday, the little Printer devil barred my door and I could not come out as I should have liked very much to meet Colonel Crowstade — Colonel Newcome I mean, whom I have already had the pleasure of meeting at your house with an exterior wh. the world would call crusty.

I know of no person who is inwardly so richly endowed as M. de Crowstade.

Meeting Kinglake yesterday or (no the day before) in the Park, we agreed that I should ask you if you would be so good as to receive me at dinner, or T if your table is full, on Friday : it is the first day I have when I am disengaged.

As I am in the act of writing this very last line the post man brings me your note - but on Wednesday I am going to a party of authors: and must not be faithless to my friends & brethren. Is there still hope for me dear Miss Berry ? .

Always most faithfully yours

W M Thackeray

Edward Lear

(1812–88), the master of frolicking whimsy, was the twentieth child of an itinerant London stockbroker. A shy, frail boy, he was plagued by epilepsy but contrived to escape into the romantic poetry of Byron and the mystic landscapes of Turner. Even as a youth, Lear flirted with the verse form he later made famous, the limerick. But his real ambition was to become a great artist. From painting birds with brilliant plumage he soon turned to landscapes, perhaps with a hope of rivaling Turner. His paintings and sketches are superb, but the humorous jingles that were at first only an escape valve soon became an obsession, and in 1846, with the publication of *A Book of Nonsense*, Lear established himself as an unequaled purveyor of jovial fun. His limericks, illustrated with delectable pen-and-ink sketches, enlivened nearly every nursery in England and America.

103

Villa Emily, Sanremo.
Riviera di Genova.
5 Jan.y 1876.

My dear Mrs Tennyson,

I find an old Envelope, intended to be filled up to you thousands of years ago: (but I cannot write by lamplight in these latter days, — & the whole daylight is crowded with work, — so things constantly intentioning to write *letters never get written* ;) — & as Frank has just told me that Lionel is really engaged to Miss Locker, I shall use this ancient Letter even to send my Congratulations

34

My love to everybody.

Yours affectionately,

Edward Lear.

View in Villa Emily. Sanremo.

Lear's letters, full of his own merry, irrepressible personality, are often adorned with Arbuckle-like caricatures of himself as he cavorted with his almost equally preposterous cat, Old Foss. Like Lewis Carroll, Lear loved to invent comic words, and even in his own versified portrait he included his spoof of neologism, *runcible,* a word that perfectly describes the man and his work:

How pleasant to know
   Mr. Lear
  Who has written such
    volumes of stuff:
Some think him ill-tempered
  and queer,
  But a few think him
    pleasant enough . . .

He has many friends,
   laymen and clerical,
  Old Foss is the name of
   his cat.
His body is perfectly
   spherical,
  He weareth a runcible
   hat . . .

He reads but he cannot
   speak Spanish,
  He cannot abide
   ginger-beer:
Ere the days of his
   pilgrimage vanish,
  How pleasant to know
   Mr. Lear!

Glenfinlas. 16th October. 1853

My dear Furnivall.

I have been living so idle a life for the last month or two that the laziness has become quite inveterate — and I can't so much as write you a letter — except to answer your kind questions. We have been since 5th July living in this kind of house — with a little garden about eighteen feet long by ten wide, sloping down the bank in front — and part of Ben Ledi sloping up (among the writing) behind. — a bog in front — a wonderful working dingle in the distance at A. where Millais is painting a picture of a torrent among rocks — which will make a revolution in landscape painting. if he can only get it finished. It is not nearly done yet — and the cold is coming fast on. I am to lecture in Edinburgh — 1st November to 11th. I hope to be home before Xmas — but shall linger on the road. though it is

John Ruskin

(1819–1900), as a boy, looked upon himself as a rare genius, destined to be a combination bishop and poet. But, despite a superb aesthetic education, he was an indifferent Latin scholar. At twenty-four he was finally graduated from Oxford and immediately embarked upon a defense of J. M. W. Turner that inflamed the British art critics. Ruskin turned to architecture and wrote *The Stones of Venice,* described by Carlyle as "a new Renaissance." From this point on, Ruskin, actually a skilled artist who eschewed the palette and the easel, devoted his great talents to preaching—no other word describes the moral intensity of his essays—on art, education, morals, social problems, and any other subject that irritated or inspired him. Ruskin's peppery "sermons" won wide acclaim. He was elected a professor at Oxford in 1869 and near the close of his long life was loaded with honorary degrees.

In this letter to Frederick J. Furnivall, the English critic and editor, Ruskin describes his countryside cottage near which John Everett Millais is painting a picture of a torrent among rocks which "will make a revolution in landscape painting . . ."

Richard Burton (1821–90) was called "half-god, half-devil" by the president of the Royal Geographical Society. And the poet Swinburne, in a funeral elegy, said, "Burton's life was more exciting than any tale to be found in *The Arabian Nights*." Burton was born of English parents in Ireland and joined the British army in India in 1842. From that day he led a life of high adventure and intrigue. At thirty-three he was England's most notorious lover, broadsword champion of Europe, an expert pistol shot, and an accomplished horseman. He spoke Arabic so fluently that after dyeing his skin brown (it took several years for the dye to wear off) he was able to join a caravan traveling to Mecca, the forbidden holy city of Islam. There he actually measured the sacred Kaaba, although instant death would have awaited him if he had been discovered to be a Christian.

During a trip into Africa, Burton and his associate John Hanning Speke repelled a surprise attack of 350 savage Somali warriors. Burton was struck in the cheek with a spear and fought his way out of the ring of attackers with the spear still impaled in his jaw. Two years later, in search of the sources of the Nile, he and Speke penetrated unexplored Central Africa as far as Lake Tanganyika. Burton translated *The Arabian Nights* as well as many erotic Oriental works. His narratives of travel are among the most exciting of their type ever written. He was knighted by Queen Victoria in 1886.

When Burton's assertions were challenged by a learned member of the Royal Geographical Society, he replied with the textless letter reproduced here. The original letter was destroyed by its recipient, but I have reconstructed the missive precisely as it was described by those who saw it. The salutation and "complimentary close," together with the signature, are in Burton's own hand.

H. G. Wells

(1866–1946) was a phenomenon almost from the bassinet. Grants, scholarships, and honors wafted this brilliant son of a professional cricketer through school and out of London University and into a job as a science teacher. When only twenty-nine he wrote *The Time Machine,* a vivid tale that established him as a possible successor to Jules Verne. Romance after romance, all of them about time and space, comets and moons, poured out of his mind onto paper. (*The War of the Worlds* was radio-dramatized by a near-miss namesake, Orson Welles.) In 1920, Wells wrote *The Outline of History,* a ponderous work that is more notable for its unconscionable length than for its accuracy.

In this brief letter, Wells salutes the bluff William Ernest Henley, the peg-legged poet who was the model for Stevenson's Long John Silver in *Treasure Island.* After drawing an anguished caricature of himself, Wells notes: "I thought it would cheer you up a bit to know I've got the Influenza something awful.

Max Beerbohm

(1872–1956), the brilliant, irrepressible Max, has always reminded me of a great fencer who fought all his duels with a foil. Max scored innumerable touchés but never ran his victim through in the manner of James Gillray or Jonathan Swift. Born in London and educated, as were many wits, at Oxford, "the incomparable Max" acquired a reputation for cleverness even before he left college. With the impertinence of genius, he titled his first book, published when he was twenty-four, *The Works of Max Beerbohm.*

A slight, gentle, impeccably dressed man, Max knew and satirized almost every important person of his era. In 1898 he succeeded George Bernard Shaw as drama critic of the British *Saturday Review.* In 1910 he moved to Rapallo, Italy, where he dwelt in visible seclusion. He rarely answered letters. But when he deigned to reply, the Hermit of Rapallo frequently animated his letters with sketches, usually portraits, which changed them from delightful epistles into works of art.

Virginia Woolf

(1882–1941), English novelist and critic, enlivened the literature of her generation with brilliant new methods of characterization. In her short stories and novels she revealed the thoughts of her characters by the effects on them of their surroundings. Later, in such books as *The Waves* (1931), she experimented in the stream-of-consciousness technique. Much of Woolf's current popularity stems from her aggressive championship of a separate life for women.

This unusual note incorporates a self-portrait of the writer under stress and reveals an unexpected artistic talent.

Sean O'Casey

(1884–1964), a man of fierce independence fired in the crucible of a hot temper, started life as a poor Protestant lad. His father died when he was six and Sean grew up in the Dublin slums. Although he had a brief role in a Boucicault play when he was fifteen, he could find work only as a common laborer. As a workman he was wary of the idealism of the Irish nationalists and turned to Socialism. He was twenty-seven when his first article was published, but this did not mark the start of a great career, for the Abbey Theatre rejected play after play by O'Casey until, when he was forty-three, a committee of William Butler Yeats and Lady Gregory finally accepted *Shadow of a Gunman*. The play was a great success. In March 1924, *Juno and the Paycock*, a favorite of American anthologists, opened at the Abbey Theatre, and while it continued a long run to packed houses O'Casey continued to work as a laborer.

Philip Burton, Esq   19 August, 1958

Flat 3, 40 Trumlands Road, St. Marychurch, Torquay, Devon.

Tel.: Torquay 87766.

Dear Philip,
          I was very glad to hear (Paul tells me) that you had taken charge of Cockadoodle Dandy, leading him on at last where he should ha' been long ago; better late than too late. I'm sure you'll give the bird a chance to give a lusty crow, & I hope it may be a long one too.
          I have been in bed some weeks with Bronchitis which 'infiltrated' into a lung — improved aggression, & I was laid low; still am, but much better. This is why this is but a note to acknowledge your letter. Writing even this much has tired me. Several visitors are due end of week — one from Toronto, so I must rest all I can.   As ever

Sean

Flat 3, 40 Trumlands Road, St. Marychurch, Torquay, Devon.

Tel.: Torquay 87766.

"What didja say, Mr. O'Casey?"

Yeats's rejection of a new play offended O'Casey. He left Ireland forever, a volunteer exile from home, and settled in England. His reputation and fame grew, but he never gave up his principles. He turned down an honorary degree from Trinity College, Dublin. And, in his autobiography, he summarized his efforts in the struggle for human dignity with a single, final word: "Hurrah!"

O'Casey often illustrated his letters, usually with a sharp-nosed, bespectacled portrait of himself in some preposterous attitude. In this letter with a slightly shortened text, he depicts himself buried under a spate of aggressive reporters.

Victor Hugo

(1802–85), the boy wonder of the 19th-century literary world, began his incredible career with a novel, *Bug Jargal,* at age sixteen. For more than six decades he continued to pour out novels, poems, critiques, dramas, and political satires. In his own lifetime Hugo was regarded as a great lyric poet, but his verses now seem flat and trite, little more than sentimental jingles. "His books are good only to cover the foul leprosies on old walls," said Arthur Rimbaud. But this is certainly not true of Hugo's novels. Although labored and didactic, they still possess power, and in recent years a musical based on *Les Misérables* has achieved worldwide success.

It is in his art, little known and appreciated, that Hugo revealed his greatest originality. An early surrealist, he learned how to create pen spurts and blobs that probe deep into the psyche. Most of his drawings are provocative caricatures.

In this hasty pen-and-ink missive sent to a friend, the famed novelist comments on the state of literature in France: "I tell you again that our modern literature makes one shudder."

44

Roger de Beauvoir

(1809–66), one of the most exciting and colorful of French writers, started his career by casting off his real name, Edouard Roger de Bully, and pouring out a series of poems, plays, and romantic novels that caught the fancy of Paris. He lived in flamboyant luxury and in 1847 espoused an actress, Eléonore Doze, with whom he soon agreed to disagree. After a turbulent court battle that scandalized Paris, Beauvoir got a legal separation, but his mother-in-law had him imprisoned for three months and fined five hundred francs for his satirical poem *My Trial*. At last, ruined by profligacy and suffering from gout that tied him to a chair, Beauvoir died, almost forgotten, in Paris.

The illustration at the lower right depicts the noted author Barbey d'Aurevilly, whom Beauvoir describes in his letter as a Parisian Beau Brummell.

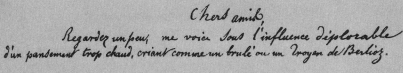

Charles Baudelaire

(1821–67) was the first great French poet to probe deep into the dark abyss of the human psyche. Born and raised in Paris, Baudelaire was nourished all his brief life on the sights and sounds of the mighty city. His greatest work, *Les Fleurs du mal (Flowers of Evil),* is a sensual and beautiful outpouring of poetic imagery. Baudelaire describes the misery of the poor, the aged, the drunk and rejected, and, above all, the wild sexual madness that raged beneath the rooftops of Paris. He ventured boldly into the unknown and perilous realm of the mortal imagination.

Tortured by his own thoughts, Baudelaire explored the artificial paradise of drugs and, after a life of dissipation, always under the evil spell of Edgar Allan Poe, he died half-crazed without ever coming to terms with himself or the world around him.

In this strange note to his publisher, Baudelaire sends two quatrains, both rough drafts, in which he gives us a verbal and pictorial glance at his tortured soul:

> . . . And my soul danced,
>   danced, a wretched scow
> Without masts, on a black
>   sea, vast and rimless

He concludes: "Take care of the different versions. I'll make the good one at your place."

François Bonvin

(1817–87), a French artist
who blossomed from a
brutal childhood, was the
son of a tough prison
guard. His mother died
when Bonvin was four and
was replaced by a cruel
and unloving stepmother.
As a small boy, Bonvin was
apprenticed to a printer. A
few years later he got a job
working for the prefecture
of police. During his few
free hours the art-loving
youth haunted the muse-
ums of Paris, especially
the Louvre, where he studied the Flemish masters.
He sketched incessantly.
Bonvin painted his friends
and enemies and trans-
formed dozens of land-
scapes into watercolors.
Eventually he began to sell
his work, but not until he
was thirty-two did he dare
to resign his job with the
police.

The warmth and vitality
Bonvin put into his paintings at first brought him
success, including the
coveted Legion of Honor.
Never able to shake off
his bad luck, however, he
spent his final years in
poor health, totally blind
and without friends.

In this little note to "my
dear Pothey," Bonvin sends
a wash drawing of a "pew
of poor wretches," hoping
that this "scrawling" will
please him.

Paul Verlaine (1844–96), raucous, boisterous, absinthe-quaffing, satyrlike, one of the great lyric poets of the world, was born at Metz, the son of an army captain who had served under Napoleon. Verlaine was educated in Paris and left school to take a menial post as clerk in an insurance company. But rhymes and liquor were already in his blood, and at twenty-two he published a little volume of delicate and beautiful "saturnian" poems that put him among the leaders of the Parnassian school of poets. New volumes of lyrics moved him closer, in thought and technique, to the Symbolists. In 1871, Verlaine acquired a drinking and rhyming companion, the audacious *enfant terrible* Arthur Rimbaud, only seventeen, who came up from the provinces just to meet and hobnob with Verlaine. Together they vagabonded over France, Belgium, and England until, in a drunken rage, Verlaine fired a pistol at Rimbaud. The youthful poet charged Verlaine with assault and Verlaine was imprisoned for two years. Upon his release from the jail at Mons, the older poet embarked on a mad, glad, bad, sad career, even assaulting his wife, who then divorced him. Verlaine eked out absinthe money by teaching English and Latin and was perpetually in and out of hospitals. He continued to write beautiful, tender lyrics. In the last years of his life, having lurched his way into immortality, the bewhiskered, snub-nosed poet, who looked like Socrates on a bender, became the greatest celebrity in the Latin Quarter.

Verlaine's letters are often illustrated, usually with scenes that incorporate a self-portrait. In this postscript from a letter he alludes to his mother, whom he once beat up, and bids farewell to a friend named Hercules, who clasps the poet in his arms.

Jean Cocteau

(1889–1963), the eternal boy of modern French literature, was a master of the fanciful, an adventurer who pursued his own youth in poetry and fiction, in art, and even in films. Cocteau captured the heart of Paris as a teenager and held it all his life. Inspired by André Gide, he dwelt in a mystical world of his own genius, yet enchanted everyone with his sophistication and charm. Like his contemporary, Salvador Dalí, Cocteau was a master of publicity. He promoted new styles and fashions and even revitalized a night club by giving it the name of one of his works, *Le Boeuf sur le toit (The Bull on the Roof).*

Cocteau created a new style of crystal-like imagery in poetry. He espoused and sponsored the music of Stravinsky and the movies of Chaplin. He was the acknowledged leader of the jet set of his day, and there was no phase of the arts that entirely escaped the magic of his touch.

50

Cocteau's pen sketches reveal an extraordinary talent. His letters sparkle with clever, appealing drawings, often provocative self-portraits. He becomes a handsome satyr, a golden young Apollo. Cocteau's artistry is chaste and powerful. A single sweeping line swiftly penned can often take us deep into his thoughts. In many of his letters, a verbal text seems almost superfluous.

In the first letter, Cocteau sends a self-portrait to Igor Stravinsky from Villefrance, October 1924: "I have a little fever and don't dare defy the germs. . ." In the second letter, also to Stravinsky, Cocteau mentions an enormous parrot that bit the composer Georges Auric, who "now plays for weddings every night. It's his only exercise. We're now hounding him for his typewriter. . ."

Jean Cocteau sends a mélange of gossip to Stravinsky. "Auric (the composer) turns his back to the sea and types on his machine. Radiguet (Cocteau's boyfriend) is dictating a novel to him. Auric and Poulenc (the composer) are telling me about the octet. I am perishing of jealousy. I'd like not to be working. Alas, we are powerless against work that loves us. Are you at work?"

In this informal pictorial note, probably to Stravinsky, Cocteau depicts some mutual friends, "nice visitors drawn to the piano." Cocteau asks: "Is Picasso at Biarritz?"

Cham's real name was a wild flurry of aigu accents—Charles-Henri Amédée, Count de Noé (1819–79). But he belied this sedate and exalted cognomen by spending his life in joyous banter. Cham was born in Paris and was thrust by his father into the Polytechnic School. He failed the final examination when he was caught making a caricature of the examiner. Cham then landed a post with the minister of finance as a sort of apprentice lawyer, but he quit because he didn't like the administration. He turned at last to art. After a stint in the atelier of Nicolas Toussaint Charlet he startled Paris with a parade of hilarious cartoons that featured the antics of naughty puppets. He was an instant success.

Although Cham's humorous sallies and even the captions to his caricatures are long outdated and his very name has been jettisoned from the encyclopedias, I still find a quaint charm in his old Parisian humor. Cham often enlivened his letters with strange creatures that gave a special zest to his gentle vagaries.

Featured here is a letter in which the improvident Cham asks his correspondent to make use of his talents, since all his money has disappeared with the trio of miscreants. He adds: "Unfortunately at this time of year one does not pass counterfeit money."

Mon Cher Monsieur

Je viens de nouveau vous demander si vous ne pourriez pas utiliser mon petit talent, vu que mes fonds ont roulé d'une manière terrible avec les gaillards ci-dessus

j'ai peut être moi même un peu aidé à l'évacuation en me donnant quelques bosses

Malheureusement à cette époque cide l'année on dépense pas mal d'argent.

Je vous serai donc bien obligé, s'il y avait moyen d'exécuter quelque choses.

Votre tout dévoué et empressé serviteur

Cham

Lorens Frölich (1820–1908), the Gustave Doré of Denmark, was born in Copenhagen and studied art in Munich, Dresden, Rome, and eventually in Paris, his adopted home. The grace and clarity of Frölich's early work quickly won him wide recognition as a painter and eventually beguiled him into his métier— book illustration. Frölich's Nordic roots drew him back to Copenhagen in 1873. He gloried in the landscape of Denmark and in a flowing, romantic style portrayed the Norse gods and the mythological heroes of Greece. His illustrations for the tales of his compatriot Hans Andersen are considered classics.

Writing to a close friend, Elie Sauvage, Frölich offers a few sketches on the antics and misadventures of his little girl. He explains that if Sauvage finds these sketches amusing, then perhaps they would please a larger public. The captions are almost as amusing as the pictures: Baby tries to earn a few sous by` working with the seamstress who is making a dress for mother. Baby finds a little friend in the mirror, so pretty that she wants to kiss her. Here's how Baby heats her iron in the front of the fireplace. She wants to iron her mother's pretty dress and while waiting she irons her doll's things. When you eat preserves you have to wash up, but you have to take precautions. "What are you up to?" "Mama, I'm embroidering."

Fontainebleau 1861 Juin

Mon cher Sauvage

— J'ai broché dans mes
moments de loisir tout un pa-
-quet d'esquisses sur des motifs
que me fournit journellement
ma petite fille; en voici quelques
échantillons, qu'en pensez vous ?

S'il est vrai qu'il faut s'amu-
-ser en travaillant pour que votre
travail puisse amuser les autres
il me semble que j'ai des chan-
-ces de plaire au public.

Tâchez donc de me trouver
un éditeur, qui ne veuille pas
tout garder pour lui. —
tout à vous   Lorenz Frölich

Bébé se souvient de son intention
de travailler pour gagner des sous; elle se
met à travailler avec la couturière, qui
fait une robe pour Maman. —

Bébé trouve la petite amie
dans la glace, si gentille
qu'elle veut l'embrasser.

Voilà, comment Bébé entend
changer son fer devant la cheminée

Mlle veut repasser la belle
robe de Maman, elle
en attendant
repasse les effets
de sa poupée

Quand on a mangé des confitures, il faut se débarbouiller; mais on doit prendre ses précautions. —

— Mais qu'est-ce que tu fais !?...
— Maman je brode. —

Gustave Castan (1823–92) portrayed the grandeur and beauty of nature, especially the majesty of the Alps. Inspired by the writings of Jean Jacques Rousseau, he developed an early love for nature. He studied art in Paris and held his first of many exhibitions in 1849 to the accolades of all the critics. A man rich in humor and amiability, Castan delighted a wide circle of celebrated friends, including Camille Corot, Théophile Gautier, and especially George Sand, whom he adored and painted. Now nearly forgotten, Castan was once regarded as a great painter of Alpine scenery, and it was said of him, "He did not copy nature; he was inspired by it."

In this pleasant letter from Geneva in 1885, with its handsome sketch of "a corner of the lake of Neuchatel du côté de Saint-Aubin," Castan tells his friend Auguste Bachelin one of the lamentable details of his life: "You ask my age. Alas, I was born in Geneva in 1823, but on December 24, and with a touch of coquetry I might say that I was born in 1824. If I were a woman I'd never miss doing it. But the truth before everything!" I can understand Castan's temptation to falsify his birthdate, for I was born precisely ninety years after Castan, on 24 December 1913, an abominable date that I cringe from, for it always makes me appear a year older than I really am.

Genève le 24 Fev. 1886

Mon cher Bachelin voici le croquis que vous me demandez. Je ne sais pas si vous pouvez en faire quelque chose — c'est un coin du lac de Neuchâtel du côté de St Aubin — Depuis que je connais mieux votre lac je trouve que c'est un de ceux où l'on trouve le plus d'études, surtout depuis qu'on a abaissé le niveau des eaux — Je ne pense pas que ceci ait été le but des ingénieurs qui ont fait ce travail, mais ils ont réussi à faire le bonheur des peintres, si ce n'est celui des riverains et surtout des [illegible] Malheureusement il y a un projet de tramway tout le long de la côte qui va complètement abîmer tous ces jolis motifs — Et les Lacustres! Qu'est-ce qu'ils vont devenir au milieu de tout cela — les vénérables tessons qui reposaient tranquillement depuis des siècles au fond de l'eau vont passer une période bien agitée.

Vous me demandez mon âge. Hélas je suis né à Genève en 1823, mais le 24 Décembre, aussi avec une grande coquetterie je puis dire que je suis né en 1824 — si j'étais une Dame je n'y manquerais pas — Mais la vérité avant tout. D'autant plus qu'il y a l'Etat Civil qui vous rappelle que vous avez un pied dans la tombe.

Tout à vous G. Castan

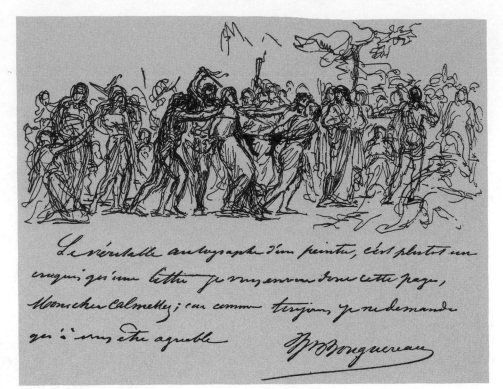

Adolphe William Bouguereau (1825–1905),

French artist, was born at La Rochelle and studied at the École des Beaux-Arts, where he won the Grand Prix de Rome. Much influenced by the art of ancient Pompeii and Herculaneum, Bouguereau painted in the grand style, turning out huge, flamboyant canvasses that delighted critics. He was the darling of dealers and collectors in his own day, but the paintings that were once bartered for enormous sums are now frowned upon as *schlock* by art experts.

In this pleasant illustrated note to a friend, Bouguereau writes: "The true autograph of a painter is rather a sketch than a letter. I therefore send you this page, my dear Calmettes, for, as always, I ask only to be agreeable to you."

Alfred Grévin

(1827–92), French carica-
turist, was the Offenbach
of the drawing board. His
gay sketches of Parisian
life won him the affection
of high society, and he
became the favorite of the
Champs Elysées. Grévin
poked fun at his contem-
poraries in an unending
stream of caricatures, all
pleasant chidings that
delighted even his victims.
So popular were his cari-
catures that he obligingly
carved them in wax. Many
of his funny creations may
still be viewed at the Musée
Grévin in Paris.

In this brief letter, Grévin
fulfills his promise to send
"a little note, a trifle, a
bit of tomfoolery," which
turns out to be a portrait
of himself, hat in hand,
laden with a huge ink pot
and gigantic quill.

Edouard Manet (1832–83)
infuriated his school teachers by filling his exercise books with sketches instead of the pedestrian problems that delight pedagogues. He studied art sporadically under Thomas Couture but kept the master in a constant growl by his independence. Manet traveled widely in Europe and finally settled down to a study of the great Spanish artists in the Louvre.

Manet quickly became a bull's-eye for the microcephalic critics of his day. They cat-and-moused every one of his paintings, nearly all of them acknowledged masterpieces. His *Spaniard Playing the Guitar* got into the Salon of 1861 but was mauled by the art experts. Two of his great paintings, despite a good word from Delacroix, were turned down by the jury.

In 1865 Manet sent to the Salon his famous *Olympia*. It was saluted by the yokel critics with sneers, hoots, and laughter. This work is now one of the jewels of the Louvre.

Every exhibition of Manet's work provoked a fresh outburst of abuse, even though he was surrounded in his later years by a coterie of admirers that included Jongkind, Fantin-Latour, and Whistler.

This and another longer letter that appears in the color section of this book were written to Mlle. Isabelle Lemonnier, a young lady Manet was sweet on.

64

Charles Altamont Doyle

This being Easter Monday. and time. to go to bed I wish to record my respectful gratitude. to the Authorities here, having a strong impression I will have no opportunity of doing so personally - and to request that my this little Sketch. Books might be sent to my poor dear wife Mary. not on account of their worth but just to shew who I was thinking of, and besides there are lots of ideas in them which under professional advice might be utilized. - that's all I've got to say - except God Bless here & the rest of them. who I dare say all forget me now. - I don't them -

HONEY SUCKLE, HOW UNLIKE ANY OTHER PLANT. BUT IT'S A CREEPER

ANOTHER SORT OF CREEPER NOT SO NICE AS THE ABOVE

in trying to go stealthily so that he has got all entangled and goodness knows how the deuce — no wonder if a feller's mind has got confused with. this fiend. and as to the angels the sooner they got away the better for themselves. —

Edouard Manet

CP 2

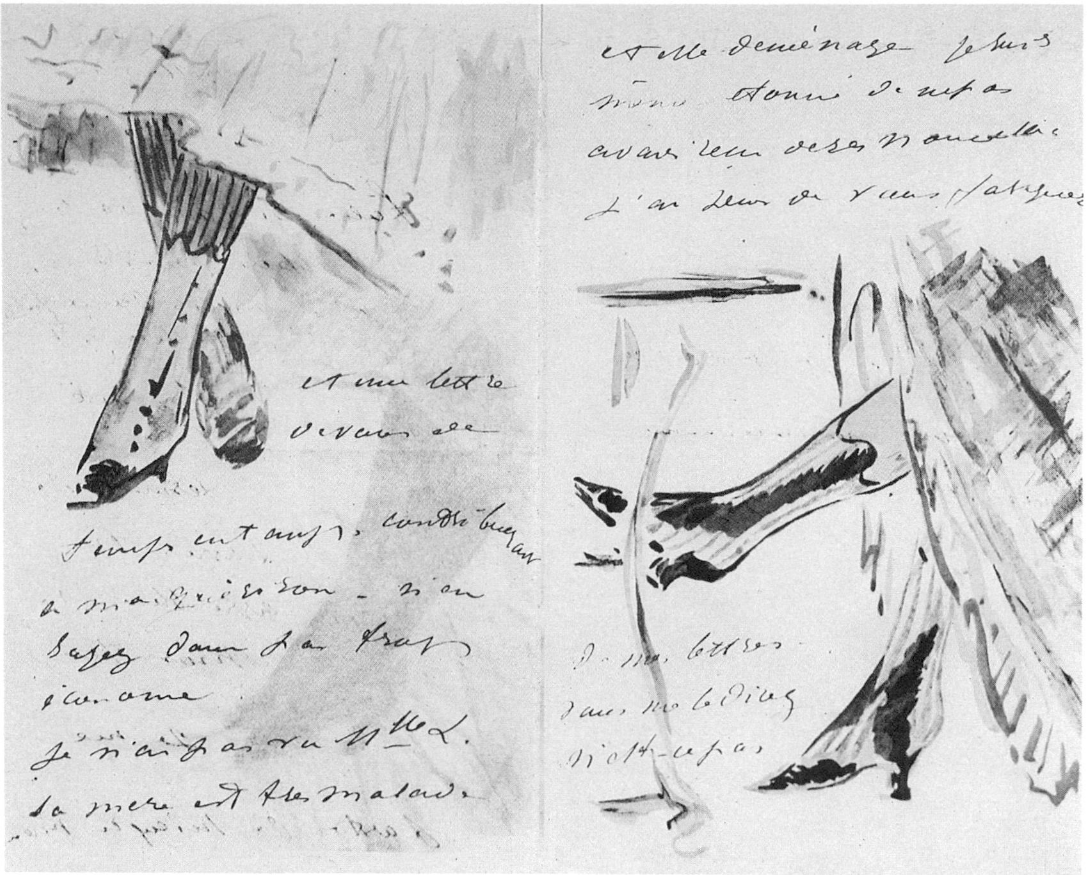

CP 3

Paul Gauguin

Février 1898 –

Mon cher Daniel.

Je ne vous ai pas écrit le mois dernier, je n'avais plus rien à vous dire sinon répéter, puis ensuite je n'en avais pas le courage. Aussitôt le courrier arrivé, n'ayant rien reçu de Chaudet, ma santé tout à coup presque rétablie c'est à dire sans plus de chance de mourir naturellement j'ai voulu me tuer. Je suis parti dans me cacher dans la montagne où mon cadavre aurait été dévoré par les fourmis. Je n'avais pas de révolver mais j'avais de l'arsenic que j'avais thésaurisé durant ma maladie d'exéma: est-ce la dose qui était trop forte, ou bien le fait des vomissements qui ont annulé l'action du poison en le rejetant, je ne sais. Enfin après une nuit de terribles souffrances je suis rentré au logis. Durant tout ce mois j'ai été tracassé par des pressions aux tempes, puis des étourdissements, des nausées à mes repas minimes. Je reçois ce mois-ci 700f de Chaudet et 150f de Manfra: avec cela je paye les créanciers les plus acharnés, et recontinue à vivre comme avant, de misères et de honte jusqu'au mois de Mai où la banque me fera saisir et vendre à vil prix ce que je possède entre autres mes tableaux. Enfin nous verrons à cette époque à recommencer d'une autre façon.

Il faut vous dire que ma résolution était bien prise pour le mois de Décembre alors j'ai voulu avant de mourir peindre une grande toile que j'avais en tête et durant tout le mois j'ai travaillé jour et nuit dans une fièvre inouïe. Dame ce n'est pas une toile faite comme un Puvis de Chavannes, études d'après nature, puis carton préparatoire etc. Tout cela est fait de chic au bout de la brosse, sur une toile à sac pleine de noeuds et rugosités aussi l'aspect en est terriblement fruste. On dira que c'est lâché etc. . . . .

D'où venons nous ? que sommes nous ? où allons nous ?

Charles M. Russell

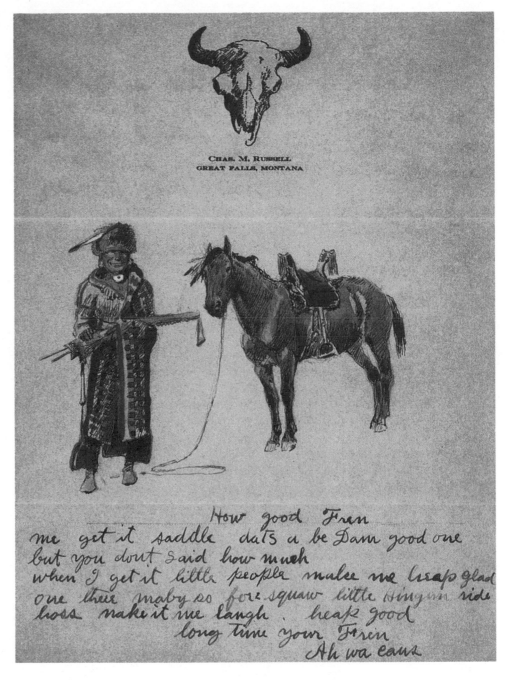

CHAS. M. RUSSELL
GREAT FALLS, MONTANA

How good Fren
me get it saddle dats a be Dam good one
but you dont said how much
when I get it little people make me heap glad
one there maby so fore squaw little Injun ride
hoss make it me laugh. heap good
long time your Fren
Ah wa caus

Charles M. Russell

November 2d
1921

Guy Weadick
T S Ranch
Longview
Alberta

Friend Guy I got your letter and am glad to here you are doing so well with your ranch it pleases me plenty to know that thair is so maney men and wimen that will quit a gas wagon and a good road and are wilen to look at the world with a horse under em . and where you live Guy if they'l step in the middel of a hoss you can show folks the top of America the wildest the bigest and for a nature lover the best part of it

In tame countrys on a good road an autos all right but if your hunting for aney thing wilder than a Doctor take a horse

I suppose by this time your on the rode I'm sending you a book which I hope you enjoy My wife and I leave for Denver tommorow morning so this is a buisy camp we will returne in about two weeks

Thanks for the Invite to viset the T S Ranch we might do that some time with best whishes to you and yours from us all Your friend C M Russell

Hendrik Willem Van Loon

To Corporal Gerard van Loon.
Class 51. Field Artillery Officers Candidate School
Fort Sill   Oklahoma.

ELEONORE POHL
HALFING in
OBERBAYERN

27. VII. 1946

PRISONER OF WAR
OSWALD POHL
NÜRNBERG
JUSTIZPALAST

XVII

MEIN LIEBES,

ES IST 12 UHR NACHTS – UND ICH GEHE NUN GLEICH ZU BETT UND DENKE, ICH SEI EIN BAUM AUS DEM SONDERBAREN BUCHENWALD. GERADE FANGEN DIE LÄDEN AN ZU SCHEPPERN, EIN STURM KOMMT AUF WIE OFT NACH SO HEISSEN TAGEN. UNSER KIND WANDERT GANZ KLEIN UND GANZ SCHNELL – WENN MAN NICHT AUFPASST – ZUR ALTEN BRÜCKE VON DER HAMMERSCHMIEDE. DA LIEGT NOCH EIN KIESHAUFEN. VON DEM HOLT ES SICH STEINE UND WIRFT SIE IN DAS WASSER UND RUFT JEDESMAL „OH". — MAN MUSS SEHR AUFPASSEN. ES GEHT AUCH GERN UNTEN INS HAUS, WEIL AUF DEM GANG SEIN LUSTGERUFE SO SCHÖN HALLT. ES RUFT DANN ALLE NAMEN, DIE ES KENNT. WENN ES AUFWACHT, HÖRT MAN'S SINGEN.

DÖRTHE AUF DER BRÜCKE AM WEHR.

KENNST DU NOCH DAS MOOR? DAHER SCHAFFEN WIR UNS DIE WARME STUBE IM WINTER.

DEINE LORE

HIER SPRINGEN DIE KINDER IN EIN AUSGESTOCHENES STÜCK UND VERSINKEN IM SCHLAMM.

UNSERE HÜTTE. DORT WURDEST DU AUCH MAL VERMUTET.

DER SCHLESIER HAT DEN LETZTEN STICH GERADE IN DEN SCHLAMM GELEGT. ER HAT NICHT VIEL VERSTAND. DA HABE ICH MIT DEN 3 FRAUEN AUS SCHLESIEN ZUSAMMEN ALLES PER KETTE UMGESCHICHTET. SIEHE - DAS SIND DIE SORGEN UNSERER TAGE.

DIE TUSCHE IST URALT UND SCHREIBT NICHT MEHR. UND ALLE DINGE SIND NOCH WIRR VERKRAHT.

LINDE PACKT ALS ENDGLIED ALLES AUF NEUE HAUFEN, WO ES TROCKENER IST.

HIER STEHT DIE ANDERE TÖCHTER VON FRAU HÖFLICH. SIE HEISST FRAU DRAGA UND IHR MANN IST VERMISST. SIE WAR MAL 7 JAHRE KINDER- FRÄULEIN.

HELLI AUF EINEM BRETT. MACHT VIELE FAXEN.

FRAU HÖFLICH, HAT 50 % ABGENOMMEN. BÄCKERMEISTERSFRAU, SEHR LIEB UND NETT.

ALLE DARGESTELLTEN GRÜSSEN, KÜSSEN TUN DICH BLOS DIE DEINEN BESONDERS

HIER HOLEN DROST UND ICH DEN TRIEFENDEN TORF AUS DEM MATSCH

TANTE KATZ. EIFRIG, SCHILT VIEL, DASS BESON- DERS HELLI NICHT DEN NOTWENDIGEN ERNST AUFBRINGT.

FRÄULEIN HÖFLICH. HAT ZÖPFE BIS ZUR ERDE, RUNDLICH, ZUFRIEDENER TYP. ALLE WERDEN SEHR SCHMUTZIG

SAG, OB SIE ES DIR GEGEN: DAS TORFBLATT. DANN BEKOMMST DU MANCHMAL SO EINEN BILDERBOGEN - DAMIT DU WEISST, WIE WIR LEBEN.

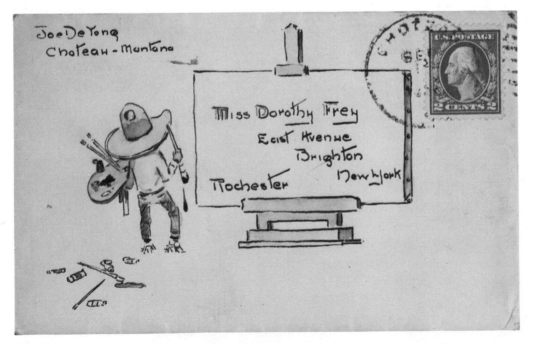

CP 12

Adolf Hitler

James Montgomery Flagg

Max Pechstein

Joseph Cornell

Paul Gauguin (1848–1903), at thirty-five, pitched aside a promising career as a stockbroker, jettisoned his wife and children, and struck out as an itinerant artist. Inspired by his friend Camille Pissarro, an Impressionist, Gauguin produced a series of brilliant but almost unsalable canvasses. For two months he lived in Arles with van Gogh.

In 1891 Gauguin sold all his paintings at auction for 9,860 francs and sailed for Tahiti, where he lived with the natives in almost abject poverty. His paintings and drawings captured the glowing warmth of the island and the smoldering beauty of its women. There he wrote his great autobiographical novel, *Noa Noa,* one of the glories of French literature.

Gauguin's letters, many of them penned to the art dealer Ambroise Vollard, are full of astute observations on his own art and the art of others. In this striking letter Gauguin sends greetings to an unknown admirer. He apologizes for the "crudity" of the beautiful sketch, suggesting for it a simple frame and if possible a glass to preserve its freshness. Another of Gauguin's illustrated letters is reproduced in the color section of this book.

Gustave Doré

(1833–83), even as a small boy in Strasbourg, in Alsace, dazzled his friends and neighbors with his remarkable sketches. At fifteen he changed his name from Paul-Gustave Dorer and struck out for Paris to make his fortune. He at once began to contribute comic drawings to Parisian periodicals and was an instant success. In 1848, the very year he arrived in Paris, he dared to exhibit some pen-and-ink landscapes at the Salon. Later, his oils and statuary won him critical acclaim, but it was as an illustrator of classics that his rampant imagination, flair for the dramatic, and artistic skill reached their zenith. Doré's powerful line drawings were an important part of my youth and in my dreams often came to life. Through his genius I galloped with Don Quixote, explored forbidden fantasies with Rabelais, sailed with the Ancient Mariner, and squirmed and sizzled in Dante's Inferno.

In these two pages from a very lengthy letter of 1866 to the widow of Gioachino Rossini, we can observe the humor and vitality in Doré's swift, incisive pen.

Vincent van Gogh

(1853–90), the son of a Calvinist pastor, began his career by working in art shops at The Hague and later in Paris and London. After a brief stint as a language teacher and bookseller's assistant, he turned to a religious career, living in humility among the miners in southwestern Belgium, where he also continued to sketch in his spare time. His affinity with the poor stayed with him all his life. By 1880 van Gogh was immersed in painting and, supported by his brother Theo, he eventually broke away from the traditions of art and began an almost savage portrayal of man and nature in brilliant colors, suffused with sunlight. The year 1888 found him in Arles, covering his canvasses with thick, pure paints that glowed with beauty. Here, for two months, he worked together with Gauguin, whom he had met in Paris.

My dear [————] for ever so long I have been wanting to write to you - but then the work has so taken me up. We have harvest time here at present and I am always in the fields.

And when I sit down to write I am so abstracted by recollections of what I have seen that I leave the letter. For instance at the present occasion I was writing to you and going to say something about Arles as it is _ and as it was in the old days of Boccaccio. -

Well instead of continuing the letter I began to draw on the very paper the head of a dirty little girl I saw this afternoon whilst I was painting a view of the river with a yellow [greenish] sky.

This dirty 'mudlark' I thought yet had a vague florentine sort of figure like the heads in the 'monticelli' pictures. and reasoning and drawing this wise I worked on the letter

I was writing to you ~~when~~ I enclose
the slip of scribbling. That you may
judge of my abstractions and forgive
my not writing before as such.
Do not however imagine I am painting
old florentine scenery – no I may dream of
such – but I spend my time in painting
and drawing landscapes, or rather studies of colour.
The actual inhabitants of this country often
remind me of the figures we see in Zola's
work.
And Manet would like them as they
are and the city as it is?
Bernard is still in Brittany and I believe
he ~~is~~ is working hard and doing well.
Gauguin is in Brittany too but has again
suffered of an attack of his liver complaint.
I wished I were in the same place with him
or he here with me.
My brother has an exhibition of 10 new
pictures by Claude Monet – his
latest works. for instance a landscape
with red ~~sun~~ set and a group of dark
firtrees by the sea side

Their temperamental incompatibility, the fierce rays of the sun, or perhaps the advancing ravages of syphilis drove van Gogh to threaten the life of Gauguin and then, by way of penitence and homage, to cut off part of his own left ear and present it to a prostitute. Wavering continuously between lucidity and craziness, van Gogh continued to paint, turning out one superb picture after another until, at last, as the darkness of insanity closed over him, he shot himself in July 1890.

Van Gogh was unrecognized by critics during his lifetime and was unable to sell his paintings, but anyone who reads his beautifully written letters, many of them illuminated with sketches, must perceive that he was extraordinarily successful as a humanitarian, a creative writer, and an artist. The failure lay in the critics of his day.

In this letter in English (June 1888) to his friend John Peter Russell, van Gogh describes what's going on in the world of art, including his own creation of a great painting.

I heard Roolin had a beautiful head at the Salon.
I have been to the seaside for a week and very likely am going thither again soon. — Flat shore sands — fine figures there like Cimabue — straight stylish. Am working at a Sower.

The great field all violet. The sky & sun very yellow. It is a hard subject to treat. Please remember me very kindly to Mrs Russell — and in thought I heartily shake hands.
             Yours very truly
                  Vincent

Paul Signac (1863–1935), born in Paris into a world of quiet, conventional art, was the son of a draughtsman who hobnobbed with many of the celebrated artists (now long forgotten) of Montmartre. By sixteen, the youthful Signac, then a student of architecture, was making copies of startling new works by Manet and Degas. With nothing but a box of paintings young Signac set up as an artist and quickly won the acclaim of the more advanced critics. Like Delacroix, whom he adored, he belonged to the cult of Apollo and was a sun worshipper. By the use of pure daubs of color he caught the prismatic beauty of light. His paintings are luminous, suffused with brilliance and clarity.

Here Signac sends a friend a few "pretty lines" that "depict the Inn of the Penjoliers, ideal for quiet."

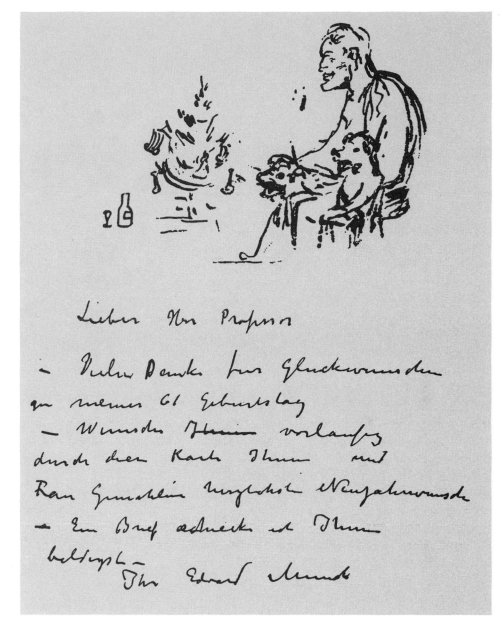

Edvard Munch

(1863–1944), the Norwegian painter and printmaker, began his studies at the School of Art and Handicrafts in Oslo. He was trained in naturalism but his genius revolted against the convention of imitating nature. Instead, he drew heavily upon the feelings of his own troubled mind. Later, his landscapes once more took on the vigor and power of realism. Many of his masterpieces hang in the National Gallery, Oslo.

In this note to Julius Meier-Graefe, art critic and early biographer of van Gogh, Munch sends thanks for greetings on his sixty-first birthday. He portrays himself with two dogs, contemplating a Christmas tree and a bottle of some solacing beverage.

Max Pechstein (1881–1955), born near Zwickau, Germany, studied at Dresden, where he began to develop the striking originality that marks his work. In 1906 he and Emil Nolde, both seeking a new and more vigorous means of art expression, joined the Dresden-based *Die Brücke* ("The Bridge") group. Influenced by Japanese art, African sculpture, Dostoevsky, and Nietzsche, *Die Brücke* was a brilliant effort to wrench loose from the traditions of the past. Although the members of the group had to battle poverty and indifference, they persisted until 1911, when they moved to Paris and soon afterward broke up. Seduced by the beauty of exotic art and the work of Gauguin, Pechstein visited the Palau Islands, where he achieved a dramatic success with his own form of expression. A well-known Expressionist, he traveled extensively in Italy and the South Seas and (after World War II) in Switzerland, Italy, and France. His paintings were branded by the Nazis as "decadent" and "harmful to the German people." In 1934 the Hitler government expelled him from the Prussian Academy and forbade him to exhibit. After the war, Pechstein moved to Berlin, where he continued to paint and teach until his death.

Pechstein's letter also appears in the color section of this book.

Marcel Gromaire

(1892–1971) was a French artist who made it his life's work to defy classification. Born at Noyelles-sur-Samre in northern France, Gromaire studied law in Paris but soon took up painting as a hobby. His plans for an artistic career were interrupted by World War I. He fought and was wounded, then volunteered as an interpreter for the American Expeditionary Forces. After the end of the war he quickly worked out his own style of art, midway between Cubism and Expressionism. Like his close friend Fernand Léger, Gromaire painted anything that came within his ken—nudes, landscapes, portraits. And he wrought his wonders in every medium—oils, watercolors, engravings, and especially tapestries. Toward the end of his long life Gromaire was almost buried in adulatory medals, blue ribbons, and gold certificates.

In this amusing letter, Gromaire sends his doctor a sketch of a terrified patient on the operating table, illustrating "the sundry motions of the condemned man." At the same time Gromaire tells his medical friend of plans for another work, a little more serious, on the same subject, presently incised "in the part of my brain bearing the inscription, 'projects.'"

75

Pablo Picasso

(1881–1973) was an artist about whom everything good and bad has already been set upon paper. There is nothing to add unless one wishes to play the piratical parrot. He was born in Malaga and studied art with his father. In 1903 he invaded Paris. A few years later he created a new type of art—Cubism. Few painters, except perhaps William Bouguereau and Sir Thomas Lawrence, have enjoyed such unanimous critical acclaim and popularity during their lifetimes. Picasso's talents appeared boundless, and almost everything that could tempt a creative artist seduced his genius. He was especially skilled in making ceramics and posters.

The epistolary scrap offered here, in which the artist sends "my dear Max" some signed papers and an amorphous comment on the weather that is "as you would expect," is decorated with blazing suns and spiderlike palms.

The wordless postcard is addressed to the art dealer Paul Rosenberg.

76

Joan Miró

(1893–1983), one of the most popular artists of modern times, was born near Barcelona and by the age of fourteen was immersed in art studies. An encounter with Picasso in Paris in 1919 swung Miró into the Cubists' camp but he soon evolved his own amoebic style of Surrealism. In 1925 Miró exhibited at the Surrealist show. An artist of great versatility, he essayed with seeming ease and always great success every form of art—murals, sets for the Ballet de Monte Carlo, ceramics, and even signed lithographs to tempt forgers.

This friendly letter expresses a hope to soon see his correspondent in Paris. The message is engulfed in Surrealistic jottings.

André Hambourg,
a brilliant French artist whose seascapes shimmer and glow with liquid beauty, was born in Paris in 1909 and trained in its finest art schools. At nineteen he held his first one-man show. Soon after the outbreak of World War II he joined the Free French Forces, serving on combat vessels as a war correspondent. He was awarded the Croix de Guerre and many other medals.

Although best known for his superb marine canvasses, Hambourg is widely acclaimed for watercolors, lithographs, ceramics, murals, and especially his sumptuously illustrated editions of modern authors.

In this letter, enhanced by a Venetian gondolier, Hambourg sends warm congratulations to his friend G.A. Masson on winning a prize.

Salvador Dali, born in 1904 in Fiegueras, Catalonia, exhibited his talent as a youth and by the time he was twenty was a distinguished book illustrator. He burst upon the New York scene by leaping through a plate-glass window to destroy what he regarded as an inept display of his work. His subsequent career was a deft meld of audacity and genius. He espoused every popular and unpopular form of creative art and was by turns a Futurist, Constructivist, Cubist, Abstractionist, and Surrealist. Dali's dazzling originality scintillates in all his art, whether motion pictures, playing cards, jewelry, book illustrations, or oils, among which the most celebrated is *The Persistence of Memory,* a landscape adorned with melting watches. Dali has achieved the ultimate form of success, that of being slavishly imitated and extensively forged on an international scale.

Here is a brief, illustrated note in fractured French, to which I have added a small display of Dali's signatures to form an ornamental border.

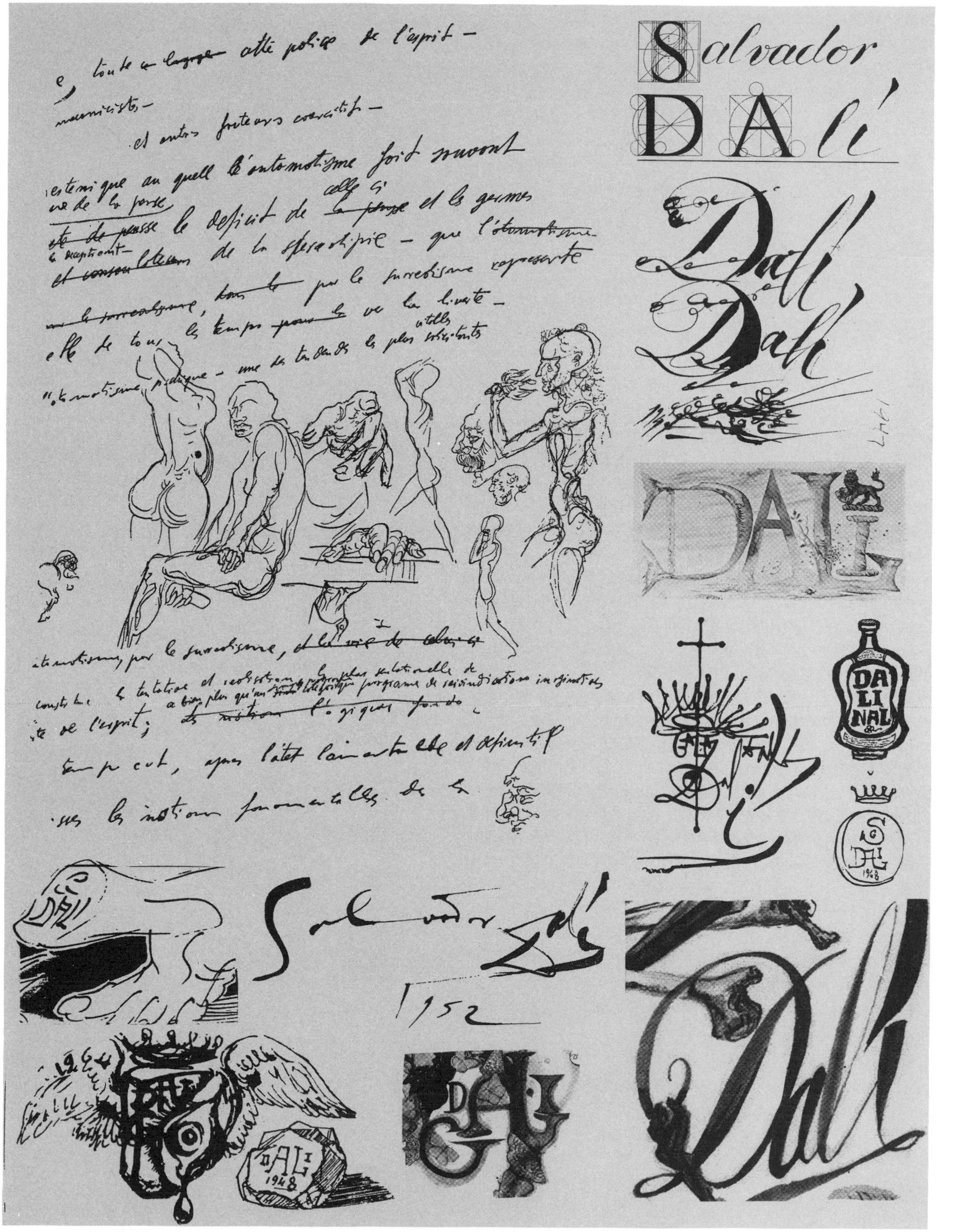
Salvador DALí
DA LI NAL
1952
DALI 1948

Benjamin Robert Haydon

(1786–1846). There never was an artist who lived more beyond his means—intellectual, financial and artistic—than Haydon. His whole life was one of precipitous folly. Yet, in the end, he attained the immortality he sought because just once in his crazy, egomaniacal career he touched the hem of Euterpe's gown. That one time was when he met and became the friend of John Keats. Haydon wrote entertainingly about Keats in his journal, painted him (with Charles Lamb and William Wordsworth) as disciples of Jesus in "Christ's Entry into Jerusalem," and further was glorified in a sonnet by Keats. Aside from his vicarious brush with the muse of lyric poetry, Haydon did little but rack up failure after failure. He had great ambitions that resulted in great disasters. Although he exhibited at twenty-one in the Royal Academy, he soon quarreled with that august institution. Twice he landed in debtors' prison. He continued to work ceaselessly on mighty canvasses that were designed, one might presume, to cover the great walls of old castles. Some of his enormous paintings won critical acclaim, but at sixty, Haydon found himself so deeply in debt and so crushed by disappointments that he scrawled the line, "Stretch me no longer on this rough world," and put a bullet into his head.

In this letter Haydon has sketched from recollection the beautiful face of the young poet John Keats.

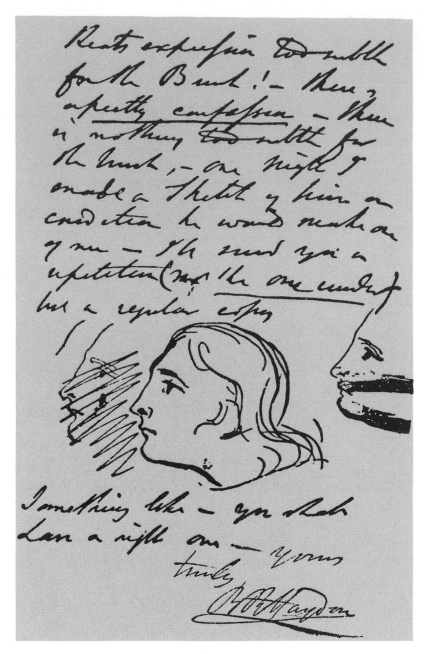

William Holman Hunt

(1827–1910), began his career in a drab warehouse office, but at sixteen his talent for drawing became so obvious that he was invited to attend the Royal Academy schools. Here he met John Everett Millais, then a boy of fifteen, who was to become his life-long friend. In 1848 he joined with Millais and Dante Gabriel Rossetti, an artist and poet, to form the famous Pre-Raphaelite Brotherhood, perhaps the dominant art force of the Victorian era. While in his twenties, Hunt became obsessed with the idea of putting Biblical stories on canvas. To that end he journeyed to Palestine, where he began a work of many years, "The Finding of Our Savior in the Temple." Completion of the painting was repeatedly delayed by anti-Semitic laws designed to prevent Jews from becoming models. Hunt's avowed ambition was "to serve as high priest and expounder of the excellence of the works of the Creator." And in this, as in other artistic efforts, he succeeded.

The letter shows Hunt in Egypt painting the tombs.

Edward Burne-Jones

(1833–98), English Pre-Raphaelite painter and designer, was born in Birmingham and educated at Exeter College, Oxford, where he met William Morris. Burne-Jones was determined to become a great artist. Under the influence of Dante Gabriel Rossetti, he left college without taking a degree. After a visit to Italy, he began turning out decorative works that soon rivaled those of his mentor Rossetti. His large oils, mostly based upon classical motifs, won him wide acclaim. He was made a baronet in 1894.

Philip Burne-Jones (1862–1926), the only son of Sir Edward Burne-Jones, whom he succeeded in the baronetcy, was educated at University College, Oxford. Sir Philip occasionally exhibited at the Royal Academy and other galleries.

May 3ᵈ. 1883.

The Grange,
West Kensington,
W.

dear Miss
Hollander —
You said you
liked letters
in the
morning. Here
is one with
nothing in it
— only a
recollection of
the Private View which
Miss Clara found so "langweilig".
Yours sincerely Philip Burne-Jones

William McConnell

(fl. 1850–65), a fun-loving caricaturist we know only through what he chose to tell us during his brief lifetime, was the son of an Irish tailor and was apprenticed to a wood-engraver. In the 1850s McConnell was appointed official cartoonist to *Punch,* the comic magazine, and *The Illustrated Times.* His style is generally touched with the bizarre and grotesque and he liked to sketch beggars and swells. He is remembered, too, for his fierce attacks on the pompous Louis Napoleon. It is reported that McConnell died of consumption.

Writing from his huge address, "17 Tavistock St." to "Dr. Friswell," McConnell promises to see his correspondent "another time." His ornate signature incorporates a palette and brushes.

Laura Knight

(1877–1970), born in Long Eaton, Derbyshire, studied at the Nottingham School of Art and first ventured to submit her work to the public in 1903, when she exhibited at the Royal Academy. Her clever studies of the circus and ballet soon won her a modest fame. In 1929 she was created a Dame of the British Empire, and in 1936 Dame Laura became the first woman academician of this century.

Her letter exhibits literary as well as artistic talent. She writes that "the catkins and pussy willows are nodding their furry heads and wagging their tails."

J. Goldsborough Bruff (1804–87), the son of a brilliant and eccentric inventor and physician, was born in Washington D.C., one of twelve talented children. His life of adventure began at ten, when the British invaded Washington. At sixteen Bruff was appointed to West Point, where he distinguished himself as an astute and clever student with a remarkable aptitude for drawing and mathematics. He was also known for his hot temper. Once, furious at a trifling insult, Bruff challenged a fellow classman to a duel and wounded him. Since duelling was a serious offense, Bruff was pitched into "the black hole" (solitary) and later, because of his popularity at the academy, was allowed to resign instead of being sacked in disgrace.

Now eighteen, Bruff got a berth as cabin boy on a merchant ship out of Georgetown. The captain took a fancy to him and for the next few years Bruff hobnobbed with rowdies and roughnecks and sailed all over the world. But after a few years before the mast, he joined his brothers at Portsmouth, where he got a government post as a draftsman.

In 1849 Bruff was lured by the cry of gold and led a company of tough characters heading across the plains for California. After many narrow escapes he returned home to his post as a draftsman, sans gold but with an illustrated journal worth many times its weight in nuggets. Bruff had recorded in meticulous and exciting detail the adventures of his company. Full of sketches, Bruff's day-to-day journal is a classic record of the gold rush.

This rebus letter to historian Peter Force is a remarkable work of art.

, March 29th: 1845

Sir,

have completed the Copy of 'Frye's Journal': satisfactory V.

Per- me, at the same, like XX my gratitude for your kind and -ly aid in the other matter.

"A in need is a in- " an old true adage.

Do hesitate command me in any way serve V.

am Sir,

With respect,

Your obliged,

O·B·D·ent,

and Very

J. Goldsborough Bruff

-script

X-QQ the of this E- .

Peter Force
Present

Thomas Nast (1840–1902), born in Landau, Germany, emigrated with his mother to New York in 1846. He studied art at the National Academy of Design and by fifteen was so skilled that he got a job sketching for *Frank Leslie's Illustrated Newspaper.* At eighteen, he joined *Harper's Weekly.* After stints as a contributing artist in England and Italy, he returned to America and won instant acclaim as a defender of the Union in *Harper's Weekly.* Abraham Lincoln called him "our best recruiting sergeant." By the late 1860s Nast, a man of great integrity and a born reformer, was hammering away at William Marcy Tweed, the Tammany Hall grafter, with clever cartoons exposing Tweed's crimes. He spurned an enormous bribe from Boss Tweed and did not relinquish his attacks until the notorious political gangster was lodged behind bars.

Nast must be ranked with James Gillray, the scourge of Napoleon, as one of the world's most brilliant and creative caricaturists. The Democratic donkey and the Republican elephant were his inventions. In addition, he transformed a skinny, rather evil-looking St. Nicholas into the jolly, fat, white-bearded Santa Claus we know today. At sixty-two, virtually wiped out by unwise investments, Nast accepted a menial appointment as consul general in Guayaquil, Ecuador, where he died of fever not long after his arrival.

Here he tells Colonel John Hay, Theodore Roosevelt's secretary of state and former secretary to Lincoln, that he is primed for departure to Ecuador: "Say the word and I am off."

Frederick S. Church

(1842–1924), born in Grand Rapids, Michigan, was at ten already sketching Indians and pirates, wild and daring men who committed fearsome deeds. At thirteen he left home to join the employ of the American Express Company, but he invested every spare moment in sketching comic scenes. At seventeen he enlisted in the Chicago Light Artillery and took part in Sherman's march to the sea. When the Civil War ended in 1865, he rejoined the American Express Company in Chicago, but after several years as the company's most inept draftsman he quit to study art in New York. Soon he was skilled enough to draw comic pictures for *Harper's Weekly,* and also illustrated a humorous almanac for the Elgin Watch Company. Church's last years were crowded with honors, and his saucy cupids and beautiful maidens, always surrounded by impudent animals, were beloved by connoisseurs of fanciful art.

Church's illustrated billets are capsule masterpieces. Nearly always confined to a single octavo page in which a drawing occupies about half the sheet, they need no interpretation other than a reading of their own text.

My Dear Mc Drake

If they don't give you Enough to eat at this Dinner Order a Welsh Rabbit on top of a Hot Mince Pie and charge to my a/c Its Fine Yours F.S. Church

Aldine Club Feby 25/1913.

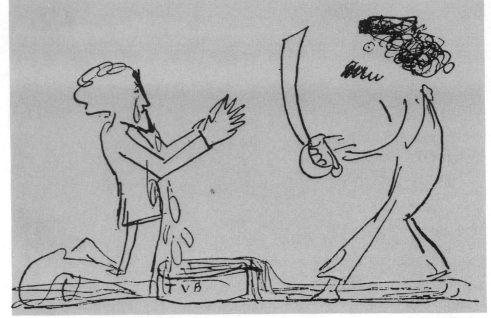

Augustus Saint-Gaudens

(1848–1907), born in Dublin, the son of a French shoemaker and an Irish mother, was brought to the United States as an infant. Apprenticed in youth to a cameo maker, he quickly exhibited his genius for capturing the human form in relief. At twenty he made a bust of his father. After five years of study in Paris and Rome, he began to dot America with his statues and medallions. They still turn up in unexpected places and delight visitors to large American cities. Saint-Gaudens's magnificent statue of Lincoln, unveiled in Chicago, reveals the nobility of the Civil War president and is considered one of the greatest triumphs of the sculptor's art. At the entrance to Central Park in New York, at 59th Street and Fifth Avenue, is his romantic statue of William Tecumseh Sherman led by a winged victory. More than any other American, Saint-Gaudens had a genius for infusing bronze with the vitality of flesh and blood.

In this eloquent apology, expressed without salutation, words, or signature, Saint-Gaudens, on his knees, begs forgiveness from Mark Twain for breaking an engagement.

92

John Singer Sargent (1856–1925),

a tall, serene, Jove-like man, was almost from boyhood marked as a genius. Born in Florence, Italy, of American parents, he got his art training in the great cities of Europe. In Paris and London the young artist showed a sharp insight into character and a suavity of style as he painted portrait after portrait. Sargent was soon looked upon by his contemporaries as a supreme master of portraiture. The affluent and the talented clamored in vain, at times, for the immortality conferred by his brush. Sargent remained untouched and aloof from the world's adulation.

This brief letter in Sargent's execrable script reads: "Here it is, my dear Duchess, the image of his father. Yours to command. John S. Sargent." And Sargent sketches a page boy holding a train.

Frederic Remington

(1861–1909), a tough, stocky young man from the School of Arts, was on the Yale football team that starred Walter Camp. The young art student quit Yale without a degree and headed West, where he wound up as a cowboy on a mule ranch. He spent more time sketching than roping. Remington's subjects, all portrayed from life, were vibrant and full of vitality, caught by the artist during some crucial or dramatic moment.

Remington wrote and illustrated books and turned out thousands of magazine illustrations, oil paintings, and bronzes. He brought the Old West to life.

Remington's letters are touched with humor, full of enthusiasm and excitement. His most trifling notes often sparkled with impromptu sketches, usually amiable caricatures of his correspondents. In this characteristic letter to "George," about an invitation to the Aldine Club to join a competition of liars, Remington draws a cartoon of George hunting, frightened out of his wits at the sudden appearance of a bird, with a second drawing of George at the club as he recounts his bravery during this encounter.

Edward W. Kemble

(1861–1933), American illustrator, best known for his sympathetic portrayals of Negro characters, began his career by illustrating advertisements. One of his ads, totally unnoticed by others, was spotted by Mark Twain, then America's greatest writer, who could have had his choice of the world's artists to add the pictorial touch to his books. Twain selected the totally unknown Kemble to illustrate his new work, *Huckleberry Finn* (1885). After a couple of false starts in which he portrayed Huck as a skulking vagabond, Kemble came up with the grinning, irre- pressible youth in a battered hat who, in the frontispiece to the first edition of *Huckleberry Finn,* holds a musket in one hand and a dead rabbit in the other. "Most rattling good," wrote Twain, and the great partnership of author and artist was bonded. Later Kemble illustrated Twain's *Pudd'nhead Wilson* and a whole series of delightful books about Negroes.

In this little note to Twain, written while Kemble was struggling with the illustrations to *Huckleberry Finn,* Kemble portrays his diffi- culties during the period when he was moving from one studio to another.

Louis M. Eilshemius (1864–1941), a poet run amuck, became a wild adventurer in the world of oils and created some of the most startling art works of his time. The son of rich parents, he was born near Newark, New Jersey, and got his initial baptism into the art world in Dresden, Germany, where he first demonstrated his skill and extraordinary powers of observation. At Cornell, Eilshemius studied agriculture to please his father, but in 1884 he transferred to the Art Students League in New York. Here Eilshemius's long life of torment and frustration started with an aborted love affair with a young temptress, Marie Fowler, for whom he wrote "Rhapsody of Regret" (1885), an erotic love poem. At the Sorbonne in Paris, Eilshemius continued his art studies and versifying. In 1887, under the pen name of Micah Enos, he published his poetic outbursts in a little volume, *A Few Culled Flowerets Scattered in a Tome.*

The lack of recognition for his creative art whipped Eilshemius into a frenzy of egomania and madness. In the belief that his tongue-twisting name had thwarted his career, Eilshemius painted for twenty-three years (1890–1913) under the abbreviated signature of "Elshemus." By 1918, he was peppering the newspapers with wild, often incoherent blasts against a world that refused to acknowledge his genius. "How can you print such slush as that Cubist disgrace of Picasso, Woman Reading a Book," he wrote. "For the Devil's sake show the public fine Art. My Art." A few years before his death, Eilshemius was struck by a car while crossing the street. He was confined to his brownstone on East Fifty-seventh Street in New York, whence he poured out his laments and malefactions against a hostile public. In his last days a modest measure of fame came to the old artist, by now "sitting among the ashes." This brought a horde of unscrupulous art dealers who stripped him of a gaslit studio full of valuable paintings and reduced him to indigence.

In this quaint letter, the pathetic artist, alone in his studio, opens his heart to an old friend: "My existence is terrible. All of last week not one soul . . ."

● *Dr. Louis M. Eilshemius, M. A.* etc.

Mightiest Mind and Wonder of the Worlds.
Supreme Parnassian and Grand Transcendant Eagle of Art.

HOURS: 10 to 11 A. M.
1 to 3 P. M.

118 EAST 57th STREET
NEW YORK CITY

In Maine.

Dear Marie Gallagher — So long that you have
not called. I wrote to Mirror 3 vrks ago —
No answer. Wrote to Rowell a week ago no
answer. Wrote to Romeike he said in answer
his readers could not find the Mirror & article story.
        Well, and you — haven't you got the
out of town papers yet? This is a mystery —
        How about selling it to other editors?
Mirror has n't done a thing about it. My existence
is terrible. All of last week not one soul. I feel
like ——. And the —— you know!!
Mch. 25/33   Au Revoir   Sincerely Louis Eilshemius

Charles M. Russell

(1864–1926), was born in St. Louis, Missouri, into a prominent, fairly wealthy family. An inept student at school who never learned, or cared to learn, how to spell, Russell had no interest in anything except drawing. At sixteen he pitched aside the social and cultural graces that were offered him and ran off to Montana to become a cowboy. Every spare moment he invested in sketching and painting. Russell was entirely self-taught and portrayed in his work only the scenes and people he knew. The youthful Russell was partial to liquor and swapped his drawings and sketches for whisky at the local bars. Eventually he quit drinking and was astonished when his oil paintings, sold for him by his wife, began to fetch what he called "dead man's prices."

Russell painted over three thousand Western scenes and sculpted at least one hundred bronzes. His style changed dramatically throughout his career, first crude, then with dark, almost somber colors, and finally with the rich, glowing palette that characterizes the great work of his final years. A simple man who viewed life in a simple way, Russell had many rustic friends who would not have been welcomed in the sumptuous drawing rooms where his paintings hung. Most of Russell's letters, many of them adorned with watercolors, were addressed to his cowboy pals. The letter and an envelope appear in the color section of this book.

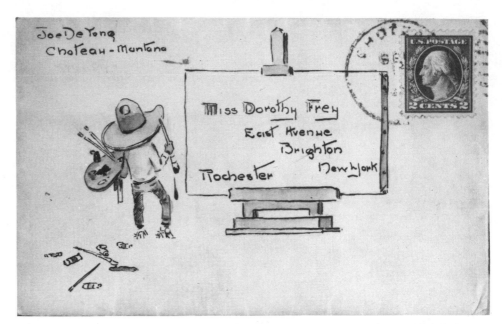

Joe De Yong,

Montana artist, must have started making marks with a pencil about the time he started making talk. "The first word I ever said, so my folks tell me, was 'horse.' I guess I've been trying to draw horses ever since then." De Yong got his first job as a cattle poke when he was just six years old. His wages were a nickel a week. By twelve he was wrangling horses and, in his spare moments, sketching. In the summer of 1912 he discovered the work of another self-taught Western artist, Charles M. Russell, and "from then on I was wild to come to Montana and meet him. I first met him in August 1914. Up to this time I had never seen an original painting." De Yong became a pupil of Russell and an intimate friend. Joe had lost his hearing during a bout with scarlet fever a year earlier, and the two men had to converse in Indian sign language.

De Yong's paintings lack the power and brilliance of Russell's. The envelopes are addressed to Dorothy Frey, a young girl who had taken a special interest in De Yong's work. They also appear in the color section of this book.

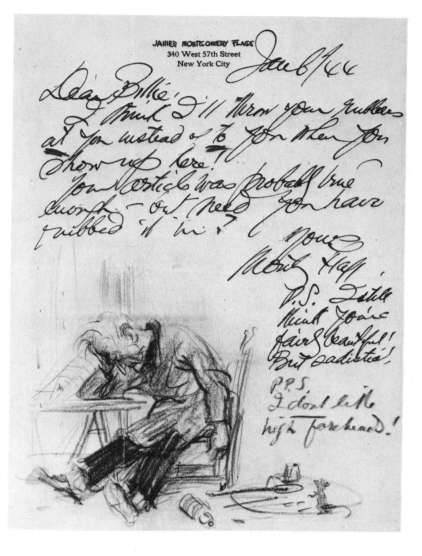

James Montgomery Flagg

(1877–1960), well known for his illustrations of strong-jawed men and beautiful girls, also is famous for his stirring patriotic posters that inspired the young men of America to gamble their lives and fortunes in two great world wars. Born in Pelham Manor, New York, Flagg was a prodigy who drew his first professional sketch for *St. Nicholas* magazine when he was only ten. At thirteen he was a regular contributor. Flagg honed his talents by four years at the Art Students League and further studies in London and Paris. He worked with incredible speed and turned out an average of two hundred and fifty pictures a year. Although a skilled portrait artist, he preferred pen-and-ink to oils. Many of his most celebrated sketches were contributed to the old-time comic magazines *Judge* and *Life*. Flagg once said that "the main difference between an artist and an illustrator is that the latter eats three square meals a day and can pay for them." Flagg's statuesque women, not unlike those of Charles Dana Gibson, often wore beautiful plumed hats that made their classic features alluringly feminine. Flagg described the ideal woman as "tall, with wide shoulders, a face as symmetrical as a Greek vase, thick, wavy hair, thick, long lashes, a wide rippling mouth and even white teeth."

In this letter he chides a woman whose article about him he found a little too candid. It also appears in the color section of this book.

Maxfield Parrish

(1870–1966), the artist who created a spectacular new shade of blue, rich as powdered lapis, to depict the color of the evening sky, was born in Philadelphia. As a small boy, young Frederick (he later took the name Maxfield) learned to sketch under the tutelage of his artist father. Parrish was intrigued by mechanical devices. He would often stare for hours at a locomotive. At Haverford College, where he studied art, he decorated the walls of his room with fancy murals of chalk and crayon, but painting soon became his sole pursuit. His creative powers blossomed at the Pennsylvania Academy of Fine Arts, and by the time he finished his studies he got his first commission, to paint the famed Old King Cole mural at the University of Pennsylvania.

Paris. Jan. 20.

I received your letter 1 hour 20 minutes and 16¾ seconds ago and I was very glad to here from you as I was expecting a letter from you or Ned for some time, why don't you write to your Buckshire—in—law sooner?

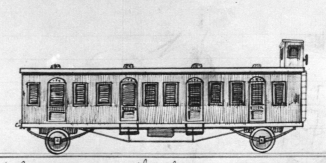

If it because you think I won't be interested
in what you tell me you are mistaken, for I like
to hear anything I can from Swarthmore or the
country round.

You ought to see the French cars, they
are enough to "give you a pain." They have a
little box on top where the brakeman sits and
takes a survey. And it is a wonder to me that
they don't run off the track as the wheels are
so far apart and are perfectly stationary.

You say the winter at home is not
much to talk about, well so it is here, nothing
but slush and mud, although lately we have had
some cold weather, and we have a daisy slide up
at school.

There is a new professor at the latter place
and he is a "holy terror", you might suppose

Travels in Europe followed, with more study, and by 1897 Parrish had his own studio and was turning out magazine covers, paintings, murals, watercolors, and drawings. Many of his widely acclaimed illustrations, like those for *The Knave of Hearts*, are now classics. For a while in later life Parrish's reputation sagged and nearly buckled, but a decade before his death at ninety-five his fame again flowered. His last years were filled with exhibitions and honors.

In this boyhood letter (about 1884) to his cousin Henry Bancroft, Parrish (who signs his name humorously as "Buck") describes his life in Paris at Dr. Korneman's school.

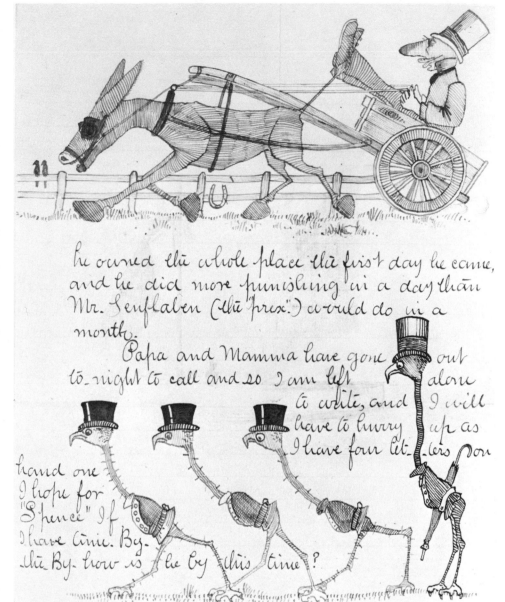

There is not mugch going on lately of
any interest except I've got the "gumps."

You fellows must have had a daisy
"christmas" didn't you, and so did I,
I did not get much of anything particular but I got a lot
of nice little reminders.
I expect you
fellows had
a nice time
up at Glou-
-ester, with
the boat
for I
know I
did at any
rate.

Box of writing paper.
Writting pad (not a clever pad)
Two candy boxes and one
big box (all vanished by this time)
Gold pin.
Pig match safe.
Compass for watch
Sleeve buttons.
David Copperfield *
Candle stick with ...
Pen holder.
Sealing wax.
Rolling Blotter, Skin shoe laces, 15 frames (3$). Lamp shade, calender
Handsome picture. St. Nickolas. Well as I am coming to
the end of the page I will have to close your Aff.
Buckshire — Buck

* you ought to read it, it's immense.

John Sloan

(1871–1951), one of the men who transformed the ashcan into a symbol of great art, was born in Lock Haven, Pennsylvania, but came to maturity in a Greenwich Village atelier. His studio soon turned into a meeting place for daring young painters. With Robert Henri and six others, Sloan exhibited canvasses of some of the sordid aspects of city life in 1908 and later in 1913. He and his associates got the name "Ashcan School," and although Sloan had painted landscapes and portraits, he devoted the rest of his long life to depicting ugly or pedestrian subjects, such as backyards, scrubwomen, and coffee lines.

A master of oils and watercolors, etchings and lithographs, Sloan was also widely acclaimed as a cartoonist and book illustrator. His letters are always very interesting. Here he agrees to illustrate a dog story and depicts himself at work encircled by an enormously long dachshund.

106

know what it is to suffer the exhaustion which results from the practice of a trade which is unlearnable — as some one said — its a disease.

My best regards to you and heres hoping we find a ready market for your story and its pictures by yours sincerely

John Sloan

Some day the Dachshund joke will be barred — till then, however, we will ring the changes

Rube Goldberg (1883–1970), a graduate of the University of California with a degree in mining engineering, belied his education and baptismal name Reuben Lucius by landing a job at the *San Francisco Bulletin* as sports cartoonist at nine dollars a week. Within a year he moved to the *Chronicle* and was pulling down five times as much, but he longed for the insanity of New York, city of the big money. Crossing the continent, Rube finagled a job at the *New York Evening Mail,* where his first cartoon series, "Foolish Questions," won him quick recognition. Soon his comic situations, catchwords like "Baloney!" and phrases like "Mike and Ike, they look alike" were cribbed by vaudeville acts. In 1924 Goldberg's "Boob McNutt" proved a palpable hit in its full-page color format every Sunday. Goldberg's glorious slapstick reached its grand climacteric with his hilarious cartoons of mechanical contrivances, such as fly swatters, so absurdly complicated that their construction would have baffled Thomas Edison.

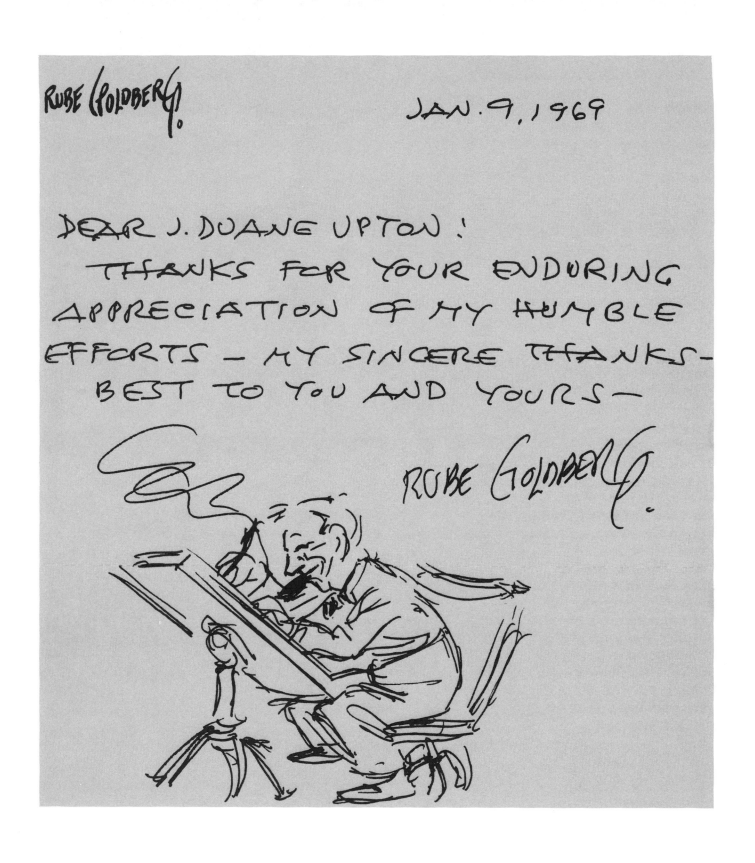

John Barrymore

(1882–1942) began his meteoric career as a cartoonist, but within a few years he outstripped his brilliant older siblings, Ethel and Lionel, to establish himself as the world's most admired stage and movie idol. Later, trapped in the Hollywood syndrome of vice and dissipation, he swapped his genius for booze and women and, in the end, little remained of him but an empty shell with a great voice.

Once that wonderful voice spoke to me. Starring on Broadway in a farce called *My Dear Children,* Barrymore blew many of his lines, but he was a brilliant improvisator, who mocked his own flamboyance. From the first row of the balcony, I was awed by his mastery of the stage. At one point he totally forgot his lines and uttered what I thought was a delectable *bon mot.* I exploded with laughter, but the rest of the packed house was silent.

Barrymore paused, held up his hand, and advanced to the apron of the stage. Looking directly at me, he bowed and said, "Thank you, my friend."

In this abbreviated letter, John Barrymore, the young art student, portrays himself at the easel. He signs with an early nickname, "Jake."

110

Joseph Cornell

(1903–73), was born in Nyack, New York, and educated at Phillips Academy in Andover, Massachusetts. At twenty-nine he stumbled upon Max Ernst's collage album *La Femme Cent Têtes,* and it changed the course of his life. He began to devise similar but far more daring creations. With no formal training he developed into a Surrealist. By 1933 he had invented a new form of art in which he created weird, suggestive tableaux inside small boxes. It was an art that a raven or magpie might have envied, for Cornell used all sorts of old bits and pieces from the past, such as sequins and cut-up illustrations, to produce sets, or series, of boxes. His collages often evoke moods of nostalgia or reverie. Two of his notable works are "Soap-bubble Set" (1948–50) and "Multiple Cubes" (1946–48).

Cornell's letter also appears in the color section of this book.

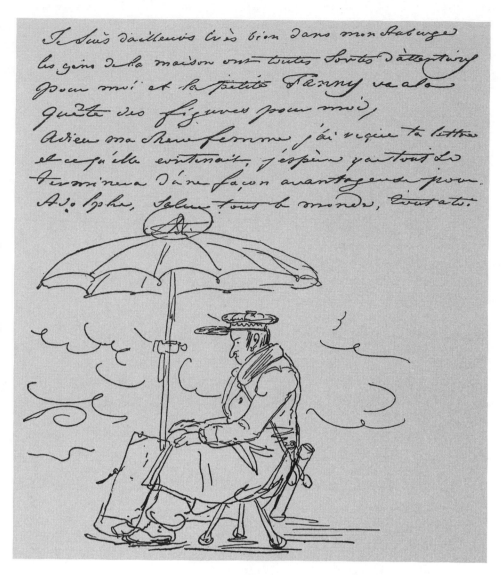

Adam Toepffer

(1766–1847), a Swiss artist, won early recognition as a printer and engraver. In his spare time he painted landscapes, but it was as a caricaturist that he eventually excelled. In 1796 at the Salon in Geneva he exhibited a collection of prominent faces on the bodies of birds. He also took time off from his printing to teach promising young artists, including Napoleon's first wife, the Empress Josephine, whom he instructed in drawing and design. A ceaseless worker, Toepffer died as he had lived, brush in hand in front of his easel.

Toepffer signs this little note to his wife with a sketch of himself, in meditation, flanked by drawing paper. So that you can observe the interesting contrast in styles between Toepffer and his famous English contemporary, W. M. Thackeray (1811–63), I have added a self-portrait of Thackeray, pencil in hand, at work beneath an umbrella.

112

E. T. A. Hoffmann

(Ernst Theodor Wilhelm Hoffmann, 1776–1822) was a master of the grotesque, with a galloping imagination, who changed his third name, Wilhelm, to Amadeus in honor of Mozart. A writer, composer, music critic, and caricaturist, Hoffmann turned out some of the most powerful tales of the romantic era. His opera *Undine* (1816) is still performed in Germany, but Hoffmann is best remembered elsewhere for the three surrealistic stories that inspired Jacques Offenbach's *Tales of Hoffmann* (1881).

Hoffman's brief life, nearly as weird as one of his own tales, wound up with the author a shuffling, wine-driven habitué of taverns.

This neatly indited letter to an actor friend, inviting him to join in a glass of excellent punch and smoke a pipe, is signed with a self-portrait.

Theodor Hosemann

(1807–75), a rollicking, tongue-in-cheek artist, was the George Cruikshank of Germany and a popular illustrator of many books for children. Born in Brandenburg, Hosemann started his career as a lithographer, then moved to Berlin to study art. His paintings of carousing and drinking parties are full of merriment. In 1857 Hosemann joined the Berlin Art Academy as a professor.

One of Hosemann's most celebrated canvasses is a family scene depicting a christening; and here, in this little rebus, he invites a friend to attend just such an event: "On Sunday, *punkt* (the black bullet, meaning punctually) 12 o'clock in the Jerusa *lamm* (lamb) *church* the *baptismal*. Afterward at my place *we will eat cherries.* For once, don't come too late. (Signed:) *Tee o Tor* (Tea O Door)."

114

Franz von Pocci

(1807–76) was a multital-
ented German artist whose
genius touched the hem
of nearly every one of the
muses. He won fame for
his humorous silhouettes
and sketches; composed
an opera and numerous
songs as well as incidental
music for marionette
shows; and, as a dramatist,
achieved success with his
folk plays.

Count von Pocci's letters
are often tiny gems and,
like the one illustrated
here, frequently begin with
a huge ornamental initial
that invites his correspondent to look, admire,
read, and relish.

Gunter Boehmer,
a jack-of-all-arts born
at Dresden in 1911, has
essayed his extraordinary
skills in painting, graphics,
illustration, landscaping,
architecture, and interior
design. In 1930 he exhib-
ited at the Dresden Aca-
demy. Through the efforts
of his intimate friend
Hermann Hesse, Boehmer
was commissioned to illustrate scores of books, a
task in which he exhibited
a marvelous variety of artistic styles. These myriad
designs have established
him as one of the most
eclectic of modern paint-
ers. In 1961 Boehmer was
appointed professor of
graphics at the Stuttgart
Academy of Design and
since then has shifted his
creative energy to large-
scale paintings, one of
which depicts a colossal
artichoke.

In this intriguing letter to
a friend, Boehmer depicts
two satyrs carrying the
massive prospectus of
a diary. He expresses his
amazement by signing
a series of exclamation
points instead of his name.

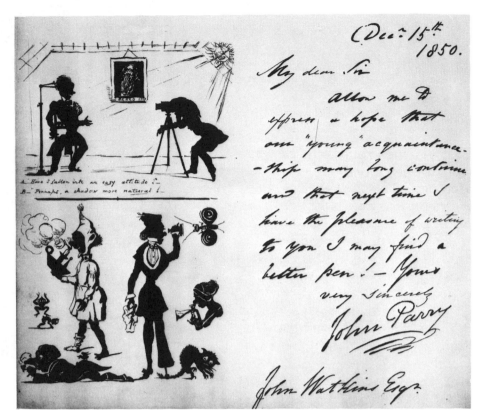

John Parry

(1812–c.1865), an English actor and amateur caricaturist, specialized in silhouette views of men, women, and animals. He was noted for his tiny silhouette profiles on the backs of visiting cards. The Victoria and Albert Museum treasures a sheet of silhouettes inscribed "Whims" that is dated in the same year as this interesting (somewhat altered) spoof on the new invention of photography.

Phiz, whose actual name was Hablot Knight Browne (1815–82), abandoned his apprenticeship as an engraver to try his skills at illustrations. The Victorian world buzzed when Boz and Phiz combined their unique talents to produce one of the most extraordinary novels of the century—*The Pickwick Papers* (1836–37). It was soon an open secret that Boz was the twenty-four-year-old literary whiz Charles Dickens, and his illustrator Phiz was only twenty-one years old. The partnership began when Robert Seymour, the first illustrator of *Pickwick,* a novel that was published in nineteen monthly installments, committed suicide in a fit of depression after an argument with Dickens. Two young men presented themselves for the ongoing job as illustrator. The rejected applicant, W. M. Thackeray (age twenty-five), was so annoyed that Dickens had selected his rival that he turned to authorship so that he could draw pictures for his own characters.

Browne and Dickens continued their symbiosis in *David Copperfield, Dombey and Son, Martin Chuzzlewit,* and *Bleak House.* A stroke in 1867 ended the great career of Phiz. He never won the acclaim he hoped for as a serious painter, but the Royal Academy recognized his genius in 1878 by awarding him a pension.

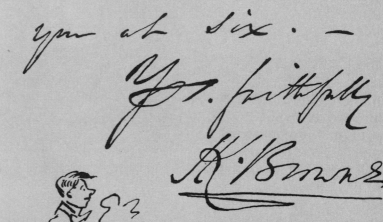

George du Maurier

(1834–96), was known wherever English was read from the moment that Trilby and Svengali burst upon a delighted—and affrighted—world. Few realized that he had been for thirty years the stellar artist of *Punch*, the English magazine of humor. Although du Maurier studied chemistry at University College, London, he quickly discovered that his métier was art. He headed for the Latin Quarter in Paris, where he'd been born. From his home on the Left Bank, the hub of the world of art, he sent forth the graphic creations that brought him a modest fame. But the Bohemian attics, then much as they had been half a century earlier in the days of Henri Murger, were awaiting the magic touch of another great romantic author. Du Maurier set himself to the task and in 1894 his novel *Trilby,* the tale of a Jewish mesmerist who created a great singer out of an ordinary chanteuse, established his reputation as a major novelist.

Du Maurier's letters are full of whimsy. When the mood was upon him he embellished his wit with clever illustrations.

Richard Doyle (1824–83), a master
of fantasy and the grotesque, was the son of
H. B. (John Doyle), a noted caricaturist whose
political satires delighted Victorian England
and whose grandson, Sir Arthur Conan Doyle,
created Sherlock Holmes. Dicky was extraordinarily precocious. He could draw before he
could write. By fifteen he had created a world
of fairyland full of whimsical, tumbling creatures. His delightful manuscript *Journal* and
his *Comic English Histories* were both written
at fifteen.

At nineteen "Dicky Bird" joined the staff
of *Punch,* the English comic weekly, and for
forty years his whimsical sketches cavorted
through the pages. Doyle's *Foreign Tour of
Messrs. Brown, Jones and Robinson* (1854)
is a Baedeker run amok, hilarious trip into
France, Belgium, and Germany that I find
even more diverting than Thackeray's
Adventures of Mr. Titmarsh.

An intimate of the great authors of Victor-
ian England, Doyle illustrated three of the
Christmas Books of Charles Dickens and
The Newcomes of Thackeray.

Dicky's boyhood letters to his father, once in
the library of his nephew Sir Arthur Conan
Doyle, are full of pen-and-ink fantasies in which
frolic the prodigalities of a youthful genius.

Sunday November 19 1843.

My Dear Father

"Look upon this picture,"

"And upon this."

My Dear Father

I think I must immediately begin a drawing on the canvass that is waiting for me up stairs, because it is really too bad to be such a long time without doing anything "important" Without meaning to say anything against my "cartoons" because I like the idea of doing them very much. yet it appears to me that if I was going on with a drawing at the same time, there would not be less done of the "cartoon" designs, while there would be much more produced in the end.   My last having been of that style of subject which cannot be described and is called "Nonsense", I would prefer doing something serious next, but whether it be an illustration of the History of England, of France. of the Low Countries, of Lord Byrons Corsair. of any of Sir Walter Scotts historical novels, of Victor Hugos Legend of Rhine, of the "Midsummers Nights Dream"; The Tempest , the "Fairie Queene". or any thing else that is interesting, it is all the same to me.   As I said before, if I am to have anything to do with the banquet whereat men on horseback attended, it would be better to make a study first in chalk on whitey-brown paper, and be quite sure of the design.   If circumstances will permit of my beginning the "cartoons" on stone directly, of course I will willingly give up everything else.

The Procession arrived upon the ground at half past one, consisting of Temperance societies banners, flowers, coaches, a band of wind instruments Father Matthew in a coach and six, and great cheering. It stopped at the edge of the precipice, which leads down into the field where the platform had been prepared (on which by the way several very fashionable ladies and gentlemen had stationed themselves), and emptying out of the vehicles prepared to descend. Without going head first this decidedly a difficult thing to do, for besides there being an immense banner in the hands of six or eight struggling men, who were quite unable to keep their feet upon the ground and it in the air at the same time, besides this, I say, the instrumentalists were disbanded, and flying down the slope like madmen in different directions, fruit women were upset, the rush of people was tremendous, the superintendants were roaring out to keep in order, ladies were screaming and falling into the ditch, the police forming in a ring round Father Mathew, fought bravely and desperately, they flung themselves back against the torrent of human beings who pressed wildly on, —but it was of no avail, hundreds were pressing from behind, there was one fruitless attempt at order, a brief but terrible struggle, a rush like a waterfall,— they are all mixed up in one dense mass,— Father Mathew, for the instant disappears and the whole mass rolls from the top to the bottom.   There is a great gasping for breath, another fierce struggle, and by degrees the head and shoulders of the reverend gentleman are seen to appear in the crowd, the band with great difficulty collect together, and strike up "see the conquering hero comes" the colors flutter in the air, and the cavalcade triumphantly march in slow time to the place of meeting amid the enlivening yells of the multitude.   Perhaps I had better pause there at this brilliant moment when the sun was shining, — — before the rain poured down and soaked

Your ~~most~~ affec~~tionate~~

Sunday January 7th 1844

My Dear Father,

I walked down Oxford Street the day before yesterday. and and as I did so, I said to myself "Can it be possible that such a thing exists as an artist who is at a loss for a character, to draw,". Because" argued I to myself if there does exist a being so degenerate only let him just put on his hat and walk out into this lively thoroughfare and watch the figures as they pass and I will undertake to say that in the course of an hour he see's more comical specimens of human nature. than he can put down in a year; the most wonderful part of the business being the contrast between every face and the one that went before it. no two. bearing the least resemblance to each other. What would not I give to have been able to sketch (as they passed me) one eighth of the intensely comical countenances that passed me bye on that day What would not I give to be able to to recollect even the half of that. Verily I do believe, to judge from what I saw that day, that nine tenths of the population of London, are the essence of fun, and such practical jokers that they dress and make remarkable faces, expressly for the amusement and gratification of such wretches as me. Cruikshank and other artists in his way, are considered very wonderful, for inventing comic figures and phiz's, and yet there are many persons, who admiring them, would not feel any amusement in contemplating the "real originals" in nature, which are a hundred times more racy and delightful than anything Cruikshank or Grandville, could do. It is all mighty fine for me to go saying that nature is better than art, just as if it is not known all over the world, but let my excuse be that, I really do imagine that some men are enthusiastic enough to think that they improve a little upon her at times.

Perhaps you have considered the matter already but if you have not I would call your attention to the extreme cheapness value and utility of the new Natural History, which under the title of Animated Nature has just commenced with the appearance of the first number. price threepence, with about fifty illustrations. the whole work to be embellished with two thousand. Besides the cheapness of the work, placing it "in the reach of the lower classes, it is sufficiently well got up. to be a desireable thing for anyone to possess to accordingly Your affectionate Son

Dick
who is fond of savage animals will "take it in".

Henry Doyle (1827–92), the third son of the caricaturist H. B., was trained as an artist in Dublin and on coming to London worked as a wood engraver for satirical journals. Often using the pseudonym Fusbos, Henry made tiny cuts for *Punch* in 1844, when only seventeen, and later revealed a fuller range of humor in his cartoons for *Fun* (1867–69). Doyle's caricatures are often miniature full-length portraits with enormous heads. Prince Albert admired his creations, and in 1869 Henry was appointed director of the National Gallery of Ireland.

Only a few of his youthful letters to his father survive. They reveal a delectable sense of banter and a jocular distortion of human form.

Sunday Morning
March 12
1842

My Dear Father

The other morning when I was
in Kensington Gardens I saw a bull finch who appeared to take a fancy
to me as far as looking went. I was going down the broad walk and I saw
a little bird on a branch of a tree, what a nice little bird said I to myself
that must be a gold finch it has yellow round its head, no it is not I remember
thinking it a curious thing when somebody told me that a Gold finch had red
round its head and that it was the Bull finch that had the yellow, then it
must be a Bull finch It seems to be watching me I will go nearer, dont be frightened
Bully, it is gone, there it is flying through the trees, what a curious motion it
flies with first rising and then sinking a little, exactly like a wave," I walk
on I have not got far when I see it again, Ah, there it is again I am sure that
is the same one what a curious thing it seems to watch me again

what a funny bird you are I wonder if he would come if I whistled, No

It does not, I declare it is singing, beautifully, what a nice bird I

wish, I could catch it, is there any way, no it is out of the question

It would be about as easy for me to catch that bird as it would be

for a rat to shoot Sir Robert Peel, I wonder if I could hit it with a

small stone, I will try, hallo, it is gone there it is flying through

the trees I know it by its waving motion, It must have seen

me stooping for a stone, what a pity I wish I had not frightened it away but it is no use, I

declare if that is not the very rogue there on that tree laughing at me so it is, How are you I

am glad to see you again, if you will just let me catch you I would say thankee, there it has

flown again I see it it has hid down behind that tree now I will have it I will get up

to the tree without it seeing me quietly now dont make a noise, I am sure it is there still

I would have seen it if it had flown away now one step more and I will — hallo there is

its head turning round the corner, if it is not making game of me I am Dick, one start forward

It is gone I cant see it any where how curious one minute it is here and the next it is no

where! well now there is no chance of me seeing it again I wish it had not gone away it

is something to do to watch it when I am by myself. Now if ever there was a curious

thing there it is again perched on the tree well I wont frighten it away this time there

it is flying along the side of the walk and perching on

trees till I come up to it, It seems to have taken a fancy to

me I wonder if it will follow me home, No now it has no

trees to hop on in front of the Palace, bother the Palace

why does not the Duke of Sussex have trees planted along in front of the Palace for birds to hop on when they want to follow me, Good bye there is no chance of my seeing you again, I must go home to my breakfast. and there ended my adventure with the Bull finch. The other morning when I came out of chapel I met Mr Safe who wanted to give me some breakfast but on my refusing on the plea that my breakfast would be waiting for me by the time I get home, then come in just to see my new Nasmyth said he, and I went in but when I had satisfied myself that the said Nasmyth was a very good landscape he renewed his attack so I gave in as the breakfast was on the table. And partook of a very pleasant meal, Mr Safe gave me a large portfolio to look over, it contained some very good engravings from the old masters some very good from Rubens a great many beautifully engraved statues which I think were out of the Musée Français, a beautiful line engraving of Wests Pyliades and Orestes in which the mellow tone of the original was wonderfully given. And a great many fine engravings of the Battles of Woavermans &ccccc. Mr Safe has got a beautiful impression of Landseers Miss Power with the dogs, it is the etching which he said he liked better than the finished Mezzotints but he was thinking of getting it slightly tinted, this Idea he said pleased Mr Watson of Bee street very much, I said that unless it was very well done indeed that it would spoil it I thought

Your affectionate

Harry

The Month is up! I have only missed one morning

PS I did not go out one morning on account of a bad toothache

PS Two mornings uncertain in as much as that we did not hear the church clock strike seven after we were out. "I love to be particular"
Vide Sir Walter Scott

Charles Altamont Doyle

(1832–93) was an inspired madman who bequeathed to the world whole folios of eerie and beautiful watercolors and sought solace in a realm of his own creation. He had spent his rather brief working life as a civil servant on a menial wage, flanked by men of mark. His father was the noted caricaturist H. B. (John Doyle), his brother was Richard "Dicky" Doyle, illustrator of Dickens, and his son was Arthur Conan Doyle, creator of Sherlock Holmes. Charles must have felt keenly his inferiority to the geniuses who surrounded him, and perhaps that is why he turned to drink. His alcoholism, combined with epilepsy, put him into a lunatic asylum at an early age. Here, like William Blake before him, he spotted fairies in trees and caught wondrous glimpses of the spirit world. Confined for many years in the Montrose Royal Lunatic Asylum in Scotland, Charles Doyle, who from boyhood had exhibited extraordinary talents as an artist, poured out his emotions in haunting pictures of enormous birds, gigantic flowers, beautiful maidens in flowing gowns, and fairies that flutter like butterflies from blossom to blossom.

In this strange letter to "the Authorities," Doyle asks that his sketch books be sent "to my poor dear wife Mary." It is also reproduced in the color section of this book. The following three pages are from a letter Charles Doyle wrote to his father.

My dear Papa

A few days ago I saw two very picturesque scenes for the first time i.e. sheep washing and sheep shearing and I was very much surprised at the manner in which the sheep underwent both operations and particularly the first although it was not a hot day but I suppose it may be accounted for by the rule that all healthy animals like water It was pitiable to see how quickly the fine old patriarchs of sheep rich in wool like this were converted into thin miserable wretches with necks so thin and giving such energetic shivers that I almost expected to see their heads dropping off there were six men engaged shearing while three more caught the sheep and one time they were bring- ing along a fine ram in triumph by one leg which required their united efforts to hold when he fell down with such a sudden jerk that he brought the three men down on him in the most degrading manner for them especially when the dog taking advantage of his masters condition set on them rooted out their faces and began to lick away with such officious good will that I have no doubt that if the ram had have waited for him he would have extended his benevolence to him also. I have just come home from the review it was the best one I ever saw and I saw it better than I generally do partly because I had a capital place and partly because I had a glass I was very near the queen saw the prince of Wales trying to sneeze suppose

it was worth seeing. cant say I saw any thing in it. I saw Sir Charles
Dalbiac thrown off his horse, that really was worth seeing, as also was
the kick which his horse delivered to the winds. I admired the
way he old man jumpt up, hope he wont have a head ack tomorrow.
I thought the rifles executed their manouvres with pluck. Prince George
seemed to think otherwise he appeared to be in a dreadful rage with
the poor colonel. "Too much of a good
thing is worse than none" I thought when
the firing began to give me a head ach.
"Disapointment sinks the heart of boy" I
said when after reading a placard about
the most extraordinary race in the world to be seen in London, I
discovered it was only a race of human beings namely Bushmen. Hope
long deferred breedeth despair I acknowleged after I had struggled for
ten minutes to get out of the crowd. One Permafathes in defering

Harry Furniss

(1854–1925), whose ink-splattered self-portrait appears here in the pudgy fingers of *The London Times* (giving him a hand!), was one of the most rollicking caricaturists of the staid Victorian era. When only a boy in London he edited a prep-school imitation of *Punch*, the famed comic magazine. Later he published a short-lived periodical that appeared to be a Chinese version of *Punch.* It was called *Lika Joko.*

After ten years as a staff artist with *Punch*, Furniss turned to book illustration, and his gently satiric drawings, sparkling with Irish wit, enlivened books by Lewis Carroll, Dickens, and Thackeray.

Many of Furniss's letters are adorned with amusing sketches. His fun-filled correspondence is always a delight to read when one can make out the wretched script.

Bruce Bairnsfather

(1888–1959), a versatile illustrator, cartoonist, and journalist, was born at Murree, India, the son of an army officer. He attended the United Service College and served with the Warwickshire Militia from 1911 until 1914, when he joined the regular Warwickshire regiment on the outbreak of World War I. With a natural talent for art, Bairnsfather turned out scores of humorous sketches of trench life replete with Cockney humor. As the Bill Mauldin of World War I he captured in his cartoons the emotions and unheroic courage of the beleaguered Tommy. His pipe-smoking "Old Bill" typified the stolid British determination. During World War II Bairnsfather was the official war artist of the United States Army in the European Theater.

In saluting the great Groucho Marx, Bairnsfather cannot resist the desire to caricature him.

THE PLAYERS
16 GRAMERCY PARK
NEW YORK CITY

Hurray! for Capt Spaulding

Dear Mr "Groucho"
I have found it difficult to refrain from drawing this impression of you, due to the sincere, understanding admiration I have, of your most-refreshing and human humor

Bruce Bairnsfather

Randolph Caldecott

(1846–86) was dubbed "Lord of the Nursery" because he drew pictures for children's books, but he was actually a very keen observer with a zesty wit, and it would be equally apt to call him "Lord of the Victorian Parlor." Caldecott was born in Chester, Cheshire, the son of an accountant. At six he was modelling in clay and wood and sketching what he saw in the countryside. At fifteen he landed a job as bank clerk in Whitchurch, a sleepy Shropshire town where, at every leisure moment, of which he had many, he continued his efforts with pen and pencil. Later he was transferred to Manchester, a city vibrant with cultural life. There, on the backs of envelopes, Caldecott sketched the depositors as they entered the bank—miser and profligate,

Davis — the American en-
graver — has not written.
with the drawings & proof-
of blocks.   I will arouse him.

As he ought
to be — I
am sure

As he is — I fear.

Yrs faithfully
R. Caldecott

the hermit and the swell. In 1869 he exhibited his first work at Manchester. Inspired by the sale of a small oil and watercolor, he quit his £100-a-year job and moved to London. His sketches caught on and before long he was famous. In only ten years he turned out a huge quantity of children's picture books that established him as a rival of Kate Greenaway. A genial, fun-filled man, Caldecott died at forty, leaving a rich legacy of illustrated letters.

Here he seeks by the deft use of two humorous sketches to rouse a slothful engraver into action. On the facing page is a self-portrait of the artist.

Kate Greenaway (1846–1901) was
born in London on St. Patrick's Day, but
that had no significance in her life or art.
She was almost pure English, with just a
tincture of Welsh, and her watercolors of
young girls in pretty bonnets depict the
beau ideal of well-behaved and proper
English children. I never look upon one of
her beguiling little girls without instantly
falling in love.

The daughter of an engraver, Kate studied
art in South Kensington and chose to special-
ize in drawing children. Her worldly success
was immediate and electrifying. Even the
ill-tempered, hypercritical John Ruskin was
seduced by her charm and praised her work.
Kate's "toy-books," as they were called,
created a revolution in book illustration.
Whimsical, quaint, humorous—these and
similar adjectives describe the costumes
in which she dressed the children of two
continents. Not only was she a skilled
artist, but the verses she wrote to go with
her delightful sketches and watercolors
show considerable poetic talent.

Kate Greenaway was famed for her modesty
and shyness, and her letters are models of
spontaneous bubbling, full of sweetness
and innocent banter. The two little letters
reproduced here were both penned to
young ladies.

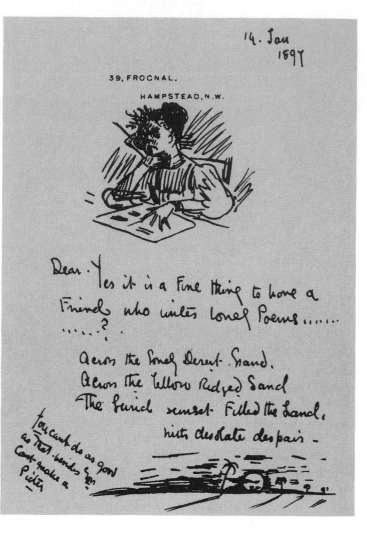

50 Frognal.
Hampstead
N.W

30 Oct
1892.

My Dear Maud.

I Trust the Remains of the Family are well.

I send you a Painty book. as I thought you might like to Paint in it also the Almanacks.

Nicts Muchs love to you

Yours affectionate

Kate Greenaway

Beatrix Potter (1866–1943), the creator of Peter Rabbit, was born in London but lived most of her life in a country cottage in Westmoreland. Even as a child she delighted in the companionship of animals. She sketched the antics of rabbits, mice, and squirrels and wrote trite nursery rhymes, like:

> My name's Mister Benjamin Bunny,
> And I travel about without money,
> There are lots I could name,
> Do precisely the same
> It's convenient, but certainly funny!

Then Beatrix began to dash off stories, little tales about animals. "I just made stories to please myself," she said years later, "because I never grew up." Her German governess got married and had a tiny son named Noël. When Noël was only five he had a long illness, and to cheer him up Beatrix wrote him "picture letters," bundles of them. They told about the adventures of Peter Rabbit and other woodland creatures. Eight years later, Beatrix got the idea that the tale of Peter Rabbit might make a little book, so she borrowed her original letter from Noël, copied it, and made it longer. Then she mailed the manuscript to a publisher, who promptly returned it. At least five other publishers turned down the most famous nursery tale of modern times. And so, in February 1900, Beatrix published the story at her own expense in a tiny edition of 500 copies. The books sold so well that Frederick Warne & Co. brought them out in a new edition with colored illustrations by the author.

Printed here is the very first Peter Rabbit tale ever written, just as Beatrix Potter wrote it in letter form to the little invalid, Noël Moore.

Eastwood Dunkeld
Sep 4ᵗʰ 93

My dear Noel,
I don't know what to write to you, so I shall tell you a story about four little rabbits.
whose names were—

Flopsy, Mopsy Cottontail

and Peter

They lived with their mother in a sand bank under the root of a big fir tree.

'Now, my dears', said old Mrs Bunny 'you may go into the field or down the lane, but don't go into Mr McGregor's garden.'

Now Flopsy, Mopsy & Cottontail who were good little rabbits went down the lane to gather blackberries but Peter who was very naughty

ran straight away to Mr McGregor's garden
and squeezed underneath the gate.

First he ate some lettuce,
and some broad beans,
then some radishes, and
then, feeling rather sick,
he went to look for
some parsley; but
round the end of a
cucumber frame
whom should he meet but Mr McGregor!

Mr McGregor was planting out young cabbages
but he jumped up & ran after Peter waving
a rake & calling out 'Stop thief'!

Peter was most dreadfully frightened &
rushed all over the garden, for he had
forgotten the way back to the gate.
He lost one of his shoes among the cabbages

and the other shoe amongst the potatoes.
After losing them he ran on four legs &
went faster, so that I think he would

have got away altogether, if he had not
unfortunately run into a gooseberry net
and got caught fast by the large buttons
on his jacket. It was a blue jacket with
brass buttons; quite new.

Mr McGregor came up with a basket which
he intended to pop on the top of Peter,
but Peter wriggled out just in time,
        leaving his jacket behind,

and this time he found the gate,
slipped underneath and ran home
safely.

Mr McGregor hung up the little jacket & shoes for a scarecrow, to frighten the black birds.

Peter was ill during the evening, in consequence of over eating himself. His mother put him to bed and gave him a dose of camomile tea,

but Flopsy, Mopsy, and Cottontail had bread and milk and blackberries for supper.   I am coming back to London next Thursday, so I hope I shall see you soon, and the new baby   I remain, dear Noel, yours affectionately

Beatrix Potter

March 5th 95.
2, BOLTON GARDENS,
LONDON, S.W.

My dear Noel,

I am so sorry to hear through your Aunt Rosie that you are ill. you must be like this little mouse, and this is the doctor

Mr Mole, and nurse Mouse with a tea-cup

I gave the elephant a lot of buns out of a bag but I did not give any to the ostriches because people are not allowed to feed them, since a naughty boy gave them old gloves & made them ill. I saw a black bear rolling on its back. I did not know that the old wolf was so good tempered. I remain yrs aff

Beatrix Potter.

A bantering letter of Beatrix Potter to young Noël Moore, then sick-a-bed.

Harrison Cady   27 West 67th Street   New York 23, N. Y.

Harrison Cady

(1877–1970), born in Gardner, Massachusetts, was one of the most endearing of artist-authors. With no more than a public school education, he began his distinguished career. His version of an adventurous rabbit, *Caleb Cottontail,* lippity-lopped into the hearts of American children. His cartoonlike watercolors, many of which I recall in *American Boy* in the 1920s, were intricately devised and when closely examined yielded many surprises.

In this epistle indited in a tiny hand, Cady apologizes for the slowness of his conveyance in returning a letter of E. B. White. The rider on the snail in none other than White's creation, Stuart Little, who cosigns the letter with Harrison Cady.

Jack Rosen a perennial optimist, was born in 1914 on the Lower East Side of New York City and graduated from P.S. 147 on Henry Street. His brother Morris, a button designer, was his earliest and most important influence. Jack boasts that he "never read a book," and his famous caricatures show a penetrating understanding of character that could not be acquired from academic studies. Rosen began to draw at age ten when he could not resist the temptation to caricature his teachers.

During a lifetime devoted to "rapid-fire" sketches—he can expose a person's strengths or weaknesses in thirty seconds—Rosen has turned out more than 100,000 drawings. Scarcely a world celebrity during the past half-century has escaped Rosen's adroit pencil, and nearly every one of them personally sat for him. Many of Rosen's sketches are now treasured in scores of American museums and libraries.

The letter reproduced here was written to me (my nickname is Bud) in 1980.

JACK ROSEN · 8701 SHORE ROAD · BROOKLYN, N.Y. 11209 U.S.A. ·· 748-3999

JULY 20, '80

DEAR BUD!

MY GRANDAUGHTER NICOLE WHO IS ONLY 3 INSISTED I DRAW ALL KINDS OF ANIMALS FOR HER, SO WE VISITED THE ILLUSTRATED ZOO.. HERE ARE SOME OF THE ANIMALS.. NICOLE LOVED THESE BUT WOULD LIKE YOU TO SHOW THEM TO YOUR CHILDREN FOR AN OPINION..... LET ME KNOW.

YOUR PAL,
JACK

Envelope addressed, in hand-lettered script:

To Corporal
Gerard van Loon
Class 51
Artillery Cadet School
Fort Sill
Oklahoma,

Postmark: NEW YORK N.Y. JAN 3 8:30 PM 1943

GRAND CENT ANNEX

3¢ UNITED STATES POSTAGE

Hendrik Willem Van Loon

Hendrik Willem Van Loon (1882–1944) sailed from his native Rotterdam for America when a small boy, but there was always a marked touch of the Dutch in him. He loved ships and Dutch history. Eventually Van Loon made a good living out of bastardizing the story of mankind and rendering it palatable with intimate fictions and delightful illustrations. He wrote a biography of Rembrandt that was actually his own life story gilded with a few facts about the great Dutch painter.

When Van Loon contemplated a book on Beethoven, he wrote to his publisher: "There won't be much about Beethoven in it. He's not very interesting. I think I'll make it my own autobiography, you know, the way I did in my life of Rembrandt."

Contemptuous of scholarship and looking upon himself as a modern-day Walter Scott, Van Loon turned out history after history, and biography after biography, illustrating them always with a plethora of brilliantly colored sketches.

In these illustrated envelopes, addressed to his son in the army, Van Loon is at his artistic best. Two others are reproduced in the color section of this book.

To Corporal Gerard van Loon. Class 51. Field Artillery Officers Candidates School Fort Sill Oklahoma

Maurice Sendak

(born in Brooklyn in 1928) is perhaps the world's most prolific illustrator of children's books. The shelves of public libraries creak with joy under the weight of dozens of his creations. As a precocious child in the adventureland of art, he designed and created his own books, filled with newspaper photos and drawings and hand-lettered and bound in colorful illustrated covers. Years later, while Sendak was working as a window decorator, some of his remarkable drawings captured the eye of a children's book editor, and young Sendak was signed up to illustrate his first book. Today there is hardly a child or young adult in America whose mind has not at one time or another been peopled by the fanciful, often surrealistic characters of this Edward Lear on a binge, many of them created to illustrate his own books.

In this little "holiday" letter he salutes a schoolmaster and his pupils.

154

Adolf Hitler (1889–1945) aspired to be a great painter. With his long, greasy hair and a scraggly beard, unkempt and unwashed and attired in a battered black derby and a caftan that reached to his ankles, he struggled to make a living as an artist in Vienna. He specialized in buildings. He had a love affair with marble and bricks. Churches were his favorite subjects. He found no beauty in fleshly curves. When he tried to paint people they looked like stuffed barley sacks. Hitler's friend Reinhold Hanisch, a petty crook and liar, peddled young Adolf's watercolors on the streets or in the bars of Vienna for a few kronen. The two men split the take and sometimes they would invest their surplus coppers in pastries at Demel's. Hitler never touched liquor. He could get high on cream puffs.

Although Hitler had twice flunked the matriculation examinations at the Vienna Academy of Fine Arts, where he had hoped to study architecture, he was determined to win a reputation as an artist. For a while he starved and slept on park benches, but eventually, aided by a few friendly Jewish art dealers, he began to sell his watercolors of the landmarks in old Vienna. In 1913 he moved to Munich to escape the Austrian draft. A year later, on the outbreak of World War I, the young artist enlisted in the German army. He took with him his brushes and paints. At the front, where he was twice wounded and once gassed, Hitler painted whenever he had a free moment. In August 1917, a thief made off with his paints and brushes. Crushed, Hitler abandoned forever his career as an artist.

Lore Pohl was the wife of Oswald Pohl (1892–1951), the notorious supervisor of concentration camps who was in charge of stealing jewelry and gold teeth from condemned victims of the Third Reich, but she clearly had no idea of the line of work her husband had been engaged in. In this pictorial letter to her imprisoned spouse, later to be hanged at Landsberg Prison on 8 June 1951, Lore writes amusingly about her life without him. Like many of the letters written by or to war criminals, this letter never reached its destination but was intercepted by a guard who brought it home from Germany as a war souvenir. It also appears in the color section of this book.

156

Index

Charles Hamilton, world leader in document authentication and forgery detection, has tracked down and helped to convict fifteen manuscript thieves and forgers. The first handwriting expert to condemn the widely publicized "Hitler Diaries" as fakes, he has published twelve books in this field, as well as several others:

In Search of Shakespeare

Leaders of the Third Reich

American Autographs

Auction Madness

Great Forgers and Famous Fakes

The Signature of America

The Book of Autographs

Big Name Hunting with Diane Hamilton

Scribblers and Scoundrels

The Robot that Helped to Make a President

Lincoln in Photographs with Lloyd Ostendorf

Collecting Autographs and Manuscripts

Braddock's Defeat

Men of the Underworld

Cry of the Thunderbird

Miró

Hendrik Willem van Loon

Edvard Munch

Beatrix Potter

Virginia Woolf

Mark Twain

C. M. Russell

1916

RUBE GOLDBERG

Victor Hugo

Paul Gauguin

E. B. J.
18 64

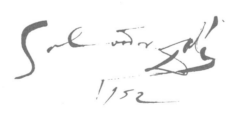

Salvador Dalí
1952

P. Signac

Baudelaire